The Writings of Jonathan Edwards
THEME, MOTIF, AND STYLE

The Writings of
Jonathan Edwards

THEME, MOTIF, AND STYLE

BY

William J. Scheick

TEXAS A&M UNIVERSITY PRESS

College Station

Library of Congress Cataloging in Publication Data

Scheick, William J
    The writings of Jonathan Edwards.

    Bibliography: p.
    Includes index.
    1. Edwards, Jonathan, 1703–1758—Criticism and
interpretation. I. Title.
PS742.S3   285.8′092′4   75-18689
ISBN 0-89096-004-6

Manufactured in the United States of America

FIRST EDITION

For
Jessica Holly

Contents

Preface

JONATHAN EDWARDS has received more critical attention than any other New England Puritan minister. His biography has been excellently told by Ola Winslow,[1] and his thought, influential in his own time, still generates interest among theologians, philosophers, and historians. Several of these more recent studies have become landmarks in our current appreciation of Edwards. The work of Perry Miller, for instance, provided insight into Edwards' thought and its relation to his time, particularly with regard to the writings of the seventeenth-century philosopher John Locke.[2] In many ways Miller's seminal work exerted such an authority that it furnished the premises for more than one subsequent study of the Puritan divine. The surprising factor in this situation is the unavoidable suspicion, on the part of anyone investigating Edwards' ideas, that Miller exaggerated their relation to Lockean notions. No one, to be sure, can deny Edwards' familiarity with Lockean concepts or his use of them in some way in his work; this fact is precisely Miller's contribution. But, as several critics have remarked, there is a need to temper considerably the view that Locke's influence on Edwards' thought was pervasive.

A perusal of New England Puritan sermons, for example,

[1] *Jonathan Edwards, 1703–1758.*
[2] *Jonathan Edwards.*

especially those written before Edwards' time, will indicate that expressions such as "the sense of the heart" and references to the "sensible" effects of grace are not unique to Edwards. The presence of these expressions in Edwards' work, consequently, cannot be readily attributed, as Perry Miller suggests, to Locke's influence. Even Solomon Stoddard, whose words time and again reverberate in the writings of his grandson, spoke of the "feeling of grace" in the heart.[3] The same is true of the expression "inward sweetness" and the honey image Edwards used to convey what he meant by "the sense of the heart." Although Locke designates sweetness as an illustration of a simple idea which the mind passively receives, the fact is that this image appears frequently in early Puritan writings, especially in those of Thomas Hooker.[4] Anne Bradstreet, to cite another instance, refers in her autobiography to spiritual "tastes of sweetness."[5] Moreover, images of honey and sweetness occur in Scripture, particularly Pss. 19:10 and 119:103, where they characterize the soul's sensation of God. The metaphor of tasting in spiritual knowledge, as Conrad Cherry has observed, was available to Edwards from Scripture, John Calvin, and the Cambridge Platonists.[6] In short, Miller was not wrong; he merely overstated the case. Lockean influences on Edwards need to be recognized, primarily the extent to which they may have caused him to be particularly sensitive to traditional images such as the ones we have just noted. Yet equally clear is the need to free ourselves from the apparent utter conclusiveness of Miller's thesis.

Miller's approach inevitably led him to read Edwards as a precursor of modern thought. This contention, in contrast to his emphasis on Locke, has proved less persuasive to most of Edwards' critics.[7] Writing from a reactionary stance, for example, historian Peter Gay remarks: "Far from being the first modern American . . . he was the last medieval American—at least among the intel-

---

[3] *A Treatise Concerning Conversion*, p. 85.

[4] See, for example, Hooker's *The Soules Vocation*, p. 47, and his *The Soules Implantation*, p. 132.

[5] *The Works of Anne Bradstreet*, ed. Jeannine Hensley, p. 243.

[6] *The Theology of Jonathan Edwards*, p. 21.

[7] A notable exception is Alan Heimert, whose enigmatic *Religion and the American Mind* reinforces Miller's view in some respects by presenting Edwards as forward looking.

lectuals."[8] Others have expressed similar, if more temperate, responses. Mason I. Lowance, Jr., has concluded that "Edwards' typology of nature is significantly medieval rather than Puritan," and Sacvan Bercovitch has cogently observed that many of Edwards' works are really "jeremiads in eighteenth-century dress, whose gradualistic apocalypticism simply provides a more effective vehicle for the old historiography."[9] Such comments are relevant to my study of Edwards because it is my belief that, although he doubtless understood the controversies of his day, he was not altogether sympathetic to the liberalizing forces. In fact, as I hope to show, he expressed a high regard for tradition—at least as he interpreted it—a respect which quite readily points to the conservatism of his later years. Edwards was a moderate with distinct conservative prejudices.

Of necessity my discussion is indebted to Perry Miller as well as to the many other students of Edwards' thought, especially whenever it has been helpful to reconsider theological matters that they have carefully analyzed. My book is, then, less an attempt at a radical departure from the mainstream of previous criticism than an effort to develop further one other angle of vision from within the established context. My primary purpose is to explore the progressive interiorization of Edwards' concerns, emphasizing its theological and artistic implications. Since, in the eyes of a Puritan, artistic features were generally seen as mere vehicles designed to convey doctrine, it is important to consider the literal content of Edwards' sermons and treatises; nevertheless, a principal interest in this study is the relevance of the artistic qualities (such broad matters as structure, motif, and style) of his writings to his doctrines.

Literary critics have by no means ignored Edwards. For the

[8] *A Loss of Mastery*, p. 116.

[9] Lowance, "Images or Shadows of Divine Things: The Typology of Jonathan Edwards," *Early American Literature* 5 (Spring 1970): 157; Bercovitch, "Horologicals to Chronometricals: The Rhetoric of the Jeremiad," *Literary Monographs, Volume Three*, p. 83. See also Vincent Tomas, "The Modernity of Jonathan Edwards," *New England Quarterly* 25 (March 1952): 60–84; Edwin Scott Gaustad, *The Great Awakening in New England*, p. 83; and Robert C. Whittemore, "Jonathan Edwards and the Theology of the Sixth Way," *Church History* 35 (March 1966): 60–75.

most part, however, they have been less successful and certainly less influential than those who have approached his work in terms of theology and intellectual history. Part of the problem is simply that Edwards did not write from that special perspective currently associated with the creative artist. Then, too, one might cite the usual arguments for explaining how Puritan culture militated against artistic expression.[10] This culture was in many respects truly deleterious to art as it is understood today. Yet, like nature, art in one form or another persisted, managing to gain a foothold in whatever crevices Puritan culture provided. It was a dwarfed, even fragile, growth, surviving the decades until it could bloom less subversively in the nineteenth century. These rudiments are evident in Puritan writings if one takes the trouble to search them out and if he treats the idea of art somewhat flexibly. Such a perspective indicates that it is as inadequate to judge much of Edwards' writing solely at the level of doctrine as it is to evaluate Ralph Waldo Emerson's essays only in terms of their literal content. Ample evidence suggests that Edwards was at times consciously concerned with technique while composing his sermons. He not only had in mind the conventional Ramist principles concerning the organization of a sermon, but he apparently conducted as well little rhetorical or literary experiments of a more inventive nature. As a minister his duty was to communicate effectively, for Puritans believed that conversion frequently occurred while one was hearing a sermon. Edwards' effort to make his sermons as effective as possible, often by means of deliberate experiments in the management of language, unveils his artistic side.

Looked at from another perspective vital to my study, language always reveals more than an author and, frequently, a reader realize. From this point of view, nonfiction becomes a legitimate subject for inquiries into the unconscious aspects of a writer's mind. Puritans thought, for instance, that the entries in one's diary revealed, in retrospect, clues to the spiritual condition of the heart, or will, the source of the very reflection recorded there. In his *Preparatory Meditations*, to cite an excellent illustration, the Puritan poet Edward Taylor time and again expressed his desire to dis-

---

[10] See Kenneth B. Murdock, *Literature and Theology in Colonial New England.*

cern in the language of his diary-like poems some indication of the spiritual state of his will.

It is, of course, difficult to say for certain whether Edwards considered his own writings in these terms. Possibly they struck him in some respects as indices of divine favor and, it follows, of his own inward condition. However this may be, the language of many of his works provides stylistic or imagistic clues to certain deep-seated feelings which he may have been disinclined to express overtly or of which he was only partially aware. *A Faithful Narrative of the Surprising Work of God*, as we shall see, represents an instance in which such intimations point to crucial features of Edwards' sentiments, strata buried beneath the exuberance of surface exposition. Thus my discussion of Edwards' artistry will take into account both conscious and unconscious aspects of his work. It is not always easy to differentiate the two, and I confess at the start that I do not often attempt to tell them apart. It seems to me less important to distinguish this or that device as conscious or unconscious than to pinpoint the actual artistic quality present in the work. I might also mention that no effort has been made in this study to probe or speculate upon the psychoanalytical implications of Edwards' language and rhetorical techniques. That is frankly a complex task which someone might undertake in the future.[11]

In this study I also relate the artistic dimensions of his writings and the complementary concern of the traditional orientation of his thought to Edwards' personal desire to determine whether he was one of God's elect. For a Puritan the answer to this question, theoretically at least, was his most important care. The problem plagued Edwards, with the consequence that a substantial number of his public writings reveal a concern over his own spiritual dilemma. The chronological review of his work in this study delineates this quest for regenerate selfhood or identity in conjunction with the progressive interiorization of Edwards' concerns. It would be a mistake, however, to expect a strictly linear and totally con-

---

[11] A step in this direction is Richard L. Bushman's "Jonathan Edwards as Great Man: Identity, Conversion, and Leadership in the Great Awakening," *Soundings* 52 (Spring 1969): 15–46, and his "Jonathan Edwards and Puritan Consciousness," *Journal for the Scientific Study of Religion* 5 (Fall 1966): 383–395. See also, with reservations, Joseph H. Crooker, "Jonathan Edwards: A Psychological Study," *New England Magazine* 2 (April 1890): 159–172.

sistent development of this search in his writings; a life is not so tractable, not even that of a Puritan divine. Yet, in general, a pattern indeed emerges. It is particularly with regard to this quest for sainthood that many of Edwards' images deserve careful attention. Especially important in this respect are those images derived from nature but used to portray the inner landscape of the self and those relating to the family but pertaining to a "collective self" within God's design for creation. Eventually, as we shall see, Edwards came to realize fully that the inner self, when it is infused with and reflects the light of special grace, provides (next to Scripture) the best revelation of divine reality.

I have already alluded to my debt to the preceding critics of Edwards' work. Although I assume full responsibility for my book, I would also like to express my thanks to Professor Wayne Rebhorn for his reading of this study with a painstaking concern only a friend could offer; to Professors Roland Delattre, J. A. Leo Lemay, and Howard Miller as well as to JoElla Doggett and Jody Hausser for their valuable comments on the work while still in manuscript; and to the University of Texas Research Institute for financial assistance in preparing the manuscript for publication. Grateful acknowledgment is also made to editors Percy G. Adams and Robert H. Hopkins, who have published portions of chapter three in different form and who have granted permission to use this copyrighted material from "Family, Conversion, and the Self, in Jonathan Edwards' *A Faithful Narrative of the Surprising Work of God*," in *Tennessee Studies in Literature*, vol. 19, Richard M. Kelley and Allison R. Ensor, eds., Percy G. Adams, guest ed., by permission of The University of Tennessee Press, copyright © 1974 by The University of Tennessee Press; and from "The Grand Design: Jonathan Edwards' *History of the Work of Redemption*," in *Eighteenth-Century Studies* 8 (Spring 1975): 300–314. My wife, Marion, provided moral support and patience, for which no expression of thanks is sufficient.

The Writings of Jonathan Edwards
THEME, MOTIF, AND STYLE

[1]

Nature and the Mind:
Early Writings

Born on October 5, 1703, Jonathan Edwards spent the first thirteen years of his life in East Windsor, Connecticut. His father, Timothy Edwards, was pastor of this community and his mother, Esther, was the daughter of the famous, influential minister of Northampton, Solomon Stoddard (1643–1729). Although a frontier village, East Windsor was a fairly settled agricultural community in which, as in most typical small New England towns of the time, religion was an integral part of daily activity. Within these relatively sedate surroundings, young Jonathan's curiosity about God and nature was nurtured. During this time he doubtless may have heard—perhaps at the dinner table—something of the controversy Grandfather Stoddard had recently provoked over who should be permitted to partake of the Lord's Supper, but most likely it did not much concern him then. How could he have intuited that the liberalizing eddies of his grandfather's practice would eventually become painfully real to him when, in later years, he would find it necessary to swim against the current of its influence?

Fortunately, several of Jonathan's early writings have been preserved. These documents reveal an alert and inquisitive mind. The precollegiate essays on spiders and the rainbow are representative of this mind, both reflecting a special sensitivity to the physical world as well as to the relation between nature and God. Nature, for Jonathan, directs one's mind to the Creator. The essay on spiders implies more than the boy may have been aware of, for in relating nature and God he conveys the impression that man in some

sense dwells outside this union, that he is an observer cut off or disfranchised from nature's reflection of divine excellence) A brief essay on being or existence as well as some notes he wrote on the
mind, composed while he was in college, tend to confirm this Calvinistic undertone. It is in his diary, however, where he wrestles
with the psychological question of his conversion rather than with
philosophic notions of being, that Jonathan initiates a line of investigation which in his later works will steadily narrow this implied
distance between man and God./To lessen this sense of separation
is crucial, for the smaller it becomes, the greater will be Jonathan's
achievement of identity and the more he will abandon a feeling of
isolation and alienation for a true sense of self defined in terms of
the divine Self.)

I. *The Observing Eye*

At the age of eleven or twelve, Jonathan wrote an essay entitled "Of Insects." That this study of the flying spider reveals his
sense of wonder about the ways of nature is particularly clear in
his expressed motivation for making the investigation. Speaking of
the "little shining webbs and Glistening Strings" seemingly "tack'd
to the Sky," he explains: "there Very Often appears at the end of
these Webs a Spider floating and sailing in the air with them,
which I have Plainly Discerned in those webs that were nearer to
my eye . . . the appearance is truly very Pretty and Pleasing and
it was so pleasing as well as surprising to me that I Resolved to en-
deavour to Satisfy my Curiosity about it."[1] The essay, however,
concerns not merely one aspect of nature but, more significantly,
the force operating behind all such phenomena. After detailing several experiments and personal observations Jonathan deduces, in
typical Puritan fashion, that in the amazing spider one sees, among
other things, the operation of divine Will or Providence. In the flying spiders, he tells us, one can discern how the goodness of the
Creator "hath not only Provided for all the Necessities but also for

[1] There are two versions of this essay. The more complete of the two, the
one to which I refer, appears in Egbert C. Smyth's "The Flying Spider—Observations by Jonathan Edwards When a Boy," *Andover Review* 13 (January
1890): 5–13. I have greatly reduced the amount of italicization originally appearing in the writings of Edwards and other Puritans quoted throughout this
study.

the Pleasure and Recreation of all sorts of Creatures." Moreover, Providential wisdom is likewise manifest in the fact that each year the spiders are drowned in the sea, which prevents overpopulation without causing the arachnids to "Decrease and so by little and little come to nothing."

From his study of the spiders Jonathan arrives at an important conclusion: nothing is "brought to Pass by nature but what is the end of those means by which it is brought to pass." The actions of nature, that is to say, assert an underlying principle of order, a perfect design which is synonymous with God's Will. Everything in nature manifests a "Great Usefullness," though man may not always be capable of perceiving it. This was a traditional view of nature for the Puritans, who looked upon nature as the Second Book, for, after the Bible—the most perfect source of divine revelation available to man—nature presents a wonderful expression of divine intent. As Edwards explains in one entry in a collection of notes he kept throughout his life, "The works of God are but a kind of voice or language of God to instruct intelligent beings in things pertaining to Himself"; these works "confirm the Scriptures, for an excellent agreement exists between these things and the holy Scripture."[2]

God's communication through nature is an invitation for man to exercise his rational faculties. The trouble is, however, that since the fall of Adam and Eve, man's rational capacity has been impaired. With his faculty of reason in such a weakened condition, man cannot expect to read the meaning of nature with clarity. Puritans adhered to this notion in one form or another well into the eighteenth century.

Yet, in spite of the fallen condition of reason, sufficient remnants of its former excellence persist, enabling men to discern something of the divine intentions expressed in nature. "Of Insects," in fact, stresses the act of seeing. It implicitly focuses on what Jonathan refers to as the "observing eye." At first the essay seems to suggest that to some extent a sympathetic relation exists between the observing eye and nature. The eye is surprised, delighted with the wonder of the natural world, and the mind it informs experiences awe. Despite this emotional nexus, however, the

[2] *Images or Shadows of Divine Things*, ed. Perry Miller, pp. 61, 70.

essay ultimately hints at something of a disjunction between the two, thereby relegating the subjective mind of the seer to a position of less power and value than it initially appeared to possess. This becomes evident, for instance, when Jonathan explains, "we Alwaies find things Done by nature as well or better than [we] can imagine beforehand." This sentiment, implied throughout the essay, indicates that in a sense nature is closer to truth or the objective reality of Providence than are the subjective thoughts of the human mind. On account of its fallen state, man's mind is to a significant extent disfranchised from the ultimate reality which gives nature its identity or meaning. The human mind is alienated from this source of definition except insofar as an onlooker it passively responds to God's revelation through nature. From its own imaginings it can at best only confirm some inkling of the truth; without the attestation of nature or Scripture, the mind lacks authority. It would be mistaken to declare at this point that young Jonathan was spurning the value of the mind; the essay itself amply testifies to the contrary. Nevertheless, even in the midst of his youthful excitement over nature, his language in this early work implies a sense of distance or gap between the subjective mind and the objective reality of the divine Will operating behind natural phenomena.

In terms of our earlier remarks, the reason why man's mind is attracted to nature lies in the fact that the latter exists in some vital relationship with its Creator. Nature is comprised of obedient secondary agents operating by inherent orderly principles that remain forever in accord with the divine Will. Natural laws function as a result of an innate inclination, a mutual attraction, keeping them in harmony with the divine purpose. Even spiders exhibit this inclination, this rudimentary "volition," whenever, for instance, "by the spiders Permission" a web is produced. The corrupted eye of the perceiving mind catches glimpses of this internal agreement, and it thereby receives intimations of its own discord, of its dependence upon misinforming fancies quite out of touch, except in a paradoxical manner, with the harmony of divine Providence. As a result of the fall, that is to say, man has forfeited nearly everything of those inherent principles which once automatically led him, as they still guide all of nature, to an accurate response to the utimate reality of God. As Edwards would explain in a later work, consequent to the fall "the world was ruined, as to man, as effectually as if it had been reduced to chaos again."[3] The phrase "as to man" is important. Nature is not actually spoiled; it only appears that way to man's degenerated sight. There now exists a lag between natural fact and the alienated mind's discovery of that fact. There is an even greater lag between the mind's perception of the fact and its realization of the divine truth toward which that fact points.

We need to caution ourselves about placing too much emphasis on this early document. It is, after all, the writing of an eleven- or twelve-year old boy. On the other hand, for a boy of his age, Jonathan possessed an acute mind, and in about a year he would enter college. Furthermore, even if Jonathan may have been unaware of some of the implications of his essay, they were nonetheless functioning at some level in his thoughts. Perhaps they represent semiconscious ideas, partly the result of the Calvinistic doctrines his father, who was very proud of his son's essay, was disseminating among the laity of East Windsor. "Of Insects" is valuable for the clues it provides to at least two major themes that will appear in some form throughout most of Edwards' later writings: his sense of the gap between God's absolute sovereignty and man's feeble dependence as well as his concern over the relationship between the objective reality of divine Will and the subjective delusions of the depraved heart.

II. *What the Sleeping Stones Dream Of*

In 1716, nearly thirteen years of age, Jonathan entered the Connecticut "Collegiate School" (later named Yale College), where he would spend four years as an undergraduate, two years as a graduate student of theology, and two more years as a tutor. While there, probably in his senior year, he became acquainted with John Locke's *An Essay Concerning Human Understanding* (1690). Dur-

---

[3] *The Works of President Edwards*, ed. Samuel Austin, 2:21. This edition is hereafter cited as *Works* (Austin).

ing his years at college, he wrote several items reflecting the influence of this work, of which his notes on the mind and on existence are good examples.[4]

The entries recorded in the document entitled "The Mind" do not comprise a systematic body of thought. They are notes— thoughts as they came to Jonathan. Consequently, several confusions and contradictions appear in the work. Yet the document is remarkable, not only for the information it divulges concerning his thinking at the time, but also for the prelude it provides to his more mature thought. Many of the ideas treated briefly in this document prove seminal to his later work.

For our purposes it is not necessary to detail the ways in which "The Mind" was influenced by and diverged from Lockean notions. Leon Howard has already excellently commented on these matters.[5] What we should note, first of all, is that on the whole the work is primarily concerned with ontology. In Jonathan's view the existence of everything in the universe depends on "some arbitrary, active and voluntary, Being." This Being is God, of course, the infinite source of all existence or life and the ultimate reality. Jonathan then makes the idealistic assertion that the "secret" of creation is that all matter, the "Substance of all Bodies, is the infinitely exact, the precise, and perfectly stable Idea, in God's mind, together with his stable Will, that the same shall gradually be communicated to us, and to other minds, according to certain fixed and exact established Methods and Laws." Jonathan is defining reality in relation to the spiritual world; nature has being only insofar as

---

[4] The influence of Locke on Edwards has been widely explored. See especially Miller, *Jonathan Edwards*; Edward H. Davidson, "From Locke to Edwards," *Journal of the History of Ideas* 24 (July 1963): 355–372; Wallace E. Anderson, "Immaterialism in Jonathan Edwards' Early Philosophical Notes," *Journal of the History of Ideas* 25 (April 1964): 181–200; Claude A. Smith, "Jonathan Edwards and 'the Way of Ideas,'" *Harvard Theological Review* 59 (April 1966): 153–174; and Leon Howard, "The Creative Imagination of a College Rebel: Jonathan Edwards' Undergraduate Writings," *Early American Literature* 5 (Winter 1971): 50–56.

[5] *"The Mind" of Jonathan Edwards*. Quotations from "The Mind" and "Of Being" are from this edition. A discussion of Edwards' notion of God alone as real is presented by William S. Morris in "The Genius of Jonathan Edwards," in *Reinterpretation in American Church History*, ed. Jerald C. Brauer, pp. 29–65.

it reflects this spiritual essence. The universe, in other words, exists only in terms of mental energy—that generated by the fixed Idea in the divine Mind as well as that involved in the passive act of perception by the human mind.

Jonathan's idealism influences his definition of supreme good or excellency, which according to him is "the Consent of Being to Being, or Being's Consent to Entity. The more the Consent is, and the more extensive, the greater is the Excellency." It follows, then, that "disagreement or contrariety to Being, is evidently an approach to Nothing . . . and the greatest and only evil." Specific implications of these ideas will play important roles in Edwards' later writings, but even in "The Mind" they serve as something of a prelude to his future study of man's two chief faculties, reason and will. The "seat of the Soul," he writes, is not only in the brain (where the rational faculties were thought to exist) but also in the heart (where the will was said to reside). Significantly, the will or heart—the terms are interchangeable—is at the center of several of the entries found in "The Mind" in which Jonathan considers those factors limiting its action: God's Will and Goodness, man's apprehension of these divine attributes, and human difficulties in consenting to them. In general, however, this document reveals little concern for such psychological matters. The human self, the question of identity, is neglected. Little else is expressed on this subject than the Lockean idea that identity is linked to consciousness. In his later writings Edwards will specifically discuss the faculties of the mind in an attempt to define the self and establish the identity of the saint's soul.

The essay on being, probably written about the same time as the notes on the mind, likewise probes the meaning of existence. In this work Jonathan portrays God as the ultimate reality, as Being or Will animating natural phenomena. God must be this basic reality, he argues, because any other conclusion is unimaginable; that is, one cannot conceive of the idea of absolute nothing, which is what must be done if he denies God as the source of being. In order to convey the impossibility of such a thought, Jonathan resorts to an image which appropriately stretches reason to its limits. He invites the reader to "think of the same that the sleeping Rocks Dream of"; only then "shall we Get a Compleat idea of nothing."

Of course we are unable to envision this; the very supposition proves antithetical to the imagery of thought—nor do rocks dream. As Jonathan explains, "we find that we can with ease Concieve how all other beings should not be, we Can remove them out of our Minds and Place some Other in the Room of them, but Space is the very thing that we Can never Remove, and Concieve of its not being. . . . all the space there was before the Creation, is God himself." God is the alpha and omega of existence. Being is in fact an emanation of God, something of God but not, as in pantheism, God Himself. Jonathan's effort in this essay to discover images which communicate to the mind even while simultaneously frustrating its rational processes—thereby giving the reader a sense of the limits of reason—is an important foreshadowing of certain experiments with language he will conduct in several of his sermons.

Similar to "Of Insects" and "The Mind," the essay on being reveals Jonathan's focus on the divine Will operating behind phenomena. He again asserts that the universe "exists no where but in the Divine mind," that its continuing existence relies on God's voluntary choice. Our failure to comprehend this fact, Jonathan notes, is further testimony to the limits of the fallen human mind, which is out of harmony with reality or God: "it tis our foolish imagination that will not suffer us to see we fancy there may be figures and magnitudes Relations and properties without any ones knowing it." Man's reason, in its postlapsarian condition, is often overwhelmed by deceptive imagination. Thus there currently exists, in a sense, a gap between the objective reality of God and the subjective perceptions of the human mind.

Central to these documents is the image of man as an observer, as seer. In "The Mind," for instance, pleasure is defined as "agreeableness to perceiving being." This emphasis is doubtless partially attributable to Jonathan's adaptation of Locke's theory that the mind receives ideas by means of the body's senses and such activities of mental reflection as perceiving and willing. This view makes man largely dependent on the world around him, reinforcing the impression conveyed in "Of Insects" that man is in some sense alienated from the ultimate source of his being in a way nature is not. That nature functions as a vehicle of divine expression to man, that as an idea in the divine Mind it communicates God's Will to him gradually, and that the perceiving human mind is a passive recipient dependent on this act make clear mankind's distance from the Creator. Since the fall, men have forfeited the intuitive knowledge of God they once had. Now they are dependent on the deceiving sensorium for an inkling of the wisdom they once possessed. This sense of distance from God is compounded by the incapacity of their corrupted rational faculties to interpret fully what the senses report. Without faith, which is a divine gift received by the elect passively, and the authority of Scripture, another gift, mankind would be doomed to ignorance and to everlasting alienation from the Creator.

It is fair to say, however, that these notes on the mind contain the seeds of Edwards' later thought, when he would increasingly lessen this impression of man's distance from God. Put another way, Edwards' idealism in this work clashes with the Lockean notion that the mind depends on the senses and on reflection for its ideas. We have noted Jonathan's idealism evident in his concept of the material world as an existence in the divine Mind. The implications of this idea are extended when he notes that human consciousness is crucial in this act of divine communication, with the result that "the Material Universe exists only in the mind . . ., that it is absolutely dependent on the conception of the mind for its existence." From the convergence of Jonathan's idealism and his Lockean empiricism there arises a strange circular tangle: the ideas of the mind depend on sensuous responses to matter that is actually only an idea of the mind. This problem is not resolved, since Jonathan is considering the mind from two points of view. However, his empiricism tends to dominate his idealism in these early writings. "The Mind" principally reports his fascination with Locke's notion of the mind's dependence on the world outside itself, an objective world providing a real context for sensation and reflection. Edwards' idealism, however, will not remain latent, for within it lay the means for spanning the distance between God and man implied by empiricism.

The predominance of Lockean influence at this stage of his thinking reinforced Jonathan's typically Puritan devaluation of the self. In its fallen state the subjective self is more often governed by the beguiling imagination than by reason. Such subjectivity is synonymous with blindness. Consequently, reality, the objective source of human existence, appears distant to man. To be sure, insofar as he has being, man shares in this reality, particularly at the level of consciousness, but his share is not as full, not as harmonious as that of nature. Dependent on nature, the identity of the human self is dwarfed. Deprived of intuitive knowledge, it derives definition from encounters with the world outside itself. It learns about itself second hand, as it were, in contrast to its source of information, which exists in some intimate informing relation to its Creator. Chiefly it discovers that there is an objective reality which, despite a few clear intimations about the meaning of life, remains for the most part as imperceptible and mysterious as the idea of primordial space. It is this portrait of the self, cut off from the very source of existence, which Edwards' idealism will later redeem.

III. *Never to Leave Searching*

The extant portion of Jonathan's diary dates from December 18, 1722, to June 11, 1735, and is in most respects typical of Puritan documents of this sort.[6] With a few exceptions, such works convey very little information about the daily activities of their authors. They were not intended to do so; rather, they were to serve as records of the ebb and flow of the soul's affections in response to the stimulus of grace or to reveal the absence of divine favor. Jonathan, like numerous Puritans before him, worried over the spiritual welfare of his soul, over whether or not he was converted.

For a Puritan, conversion—the reception of saving grace and faith—was the single most important event in one's life. Without it life was meaningless. To complicate matters, the sheer weight of such a concern inevitably caused a number of problems for the Puritans regarding the conversion experience. Such questions as what constituted the signs or the stages of conversion, whether they were ascertainable, and who had the authority to evaluate them became thorny issues afflicting them even before they left Eng-

---

[6] Edwards' diary and his resolutions appear in Sereno E. Dwight, *The Life of President Edwards*, pp. 68–106 (hereafter cited as Dwight, *Life of Edwards*); Dwight's *Life of Edwards* appeared as vol. 1 of Edwards, *The Works of President Edwards*, ed. Sereno E. Dwight, 10 vols. (the 9 vols. constituting the works proper hereafter cited as *Works* [Dwight]).

land.[7] By Edwards' time the factionalism resulting from disputes over these matters—involving, among others, Grandfather Stoddard—had increased to alarming proportions, and it is not at all certain that the term *Puritanism* means very much when applied to the ecclesiastical practices of New England in the early eighteenth century. Generally, however, conversion was understood, especially by large segments of the population of the Massachusetts Bay area and the Connecticut Valley, to be available only to those God had so predestined or elected. Normally it is preceded by a time of preparation during which the saint's reason is enlightened, his conscience convicted, and his will or heart turned toward God. Controversy existed from the first as to whether even this rudimentary scheme was accurate—whether, for instance, enlightenment and conviction necessarily preceded or were in any way preparatory for the conversion experience. All agreed, however, that of the two principal faculties of the soul, the heart or will is the more essential. It represents the whole man and from it derives the entire range of human endeavors: thoughts, words, and deeds. The will, in short, is the chief component of self, and the self achieves true identity only through the saving grace received at the time of conversion.

In spite of the sincerity of his early spiritual exercises, Jonathan did not find it easy to answer the question of whether or not he personally was one of God's chosen. In his youth he had doubted the doctrine of election. "From my childhood up," he would later explain, "my mind had been wont to be full of objections against the doctrine of God's sovereignty, in choosing whom he would to eternal life, and rejecting whom he pleased."[8] At the core of Jonathan's difficulty was his sense of self, his pride. "Pride is the worst viper that is in the heart the greatest disturber of the soul's peace, and of sweet communion with Christ," he would explain later in life in a letter: "it was the first sin committed, and lies lowest in the

---

[7] Good discussions of Puritan thinking about conversion can be found in Perry Miller, " 'Preparation for Salvation' in Seventeenth-Century New England," *Journal of the History of Ideas* 4 (June 1943): 253–286; Edmund S. Morgan, *Visible Saints*; and Norman Pettit, *The Heart Prepared.*

[8] Samuel Hopkins, *The Life and Character of the Late Reverend Mr. Jonathan Edwards,* in *Jonathan Edwards,* ed. David Levin, p. 25 (cited hereafter as *Life and Character of Edwards*).

foundation of Satan's whole building, and is with greatest difficulty rooted out, and is the most hidden, secret, and deceitful of all lusts, and often creeps insensibly into the midst of religion, even, sometimes, under the disguise of humility itself."[9] Pride is antithetical to the humble submission requisite to a belief in God's absolute sovereignty, the chief doctrine underlying the concept of predestination.

According to Jonathan, he rebelled as a child even against the authority of his parents, with the result that their counsels and instruction seemed to do him little good. At the age of twenty, he still found pride to be his nemesis, as he noted in his diary: "Although I have, in some measure, subdued a disposition to chide and fret, yet I find a certain inclination, which is not agreeable to christian sweetness of temper and conversation: either too much dogmaticalness or too much egotism." In the same year he found it necessary to resolve "Never to allow the least measure of any fretting or uneasiness at my father or mother." In more general terms, he too frequently discovered himself "ready to think that I stand by my own strength, and upon my own legs"; "I yet find a want of dependence on God, to look unto him for success." The solution to this pivotal problem, he recognized, was "Never . . . to act as if I were any way my own, but entirely and altogether God's." For Jonathan this was a difficult resolution, and, despite intimations of hope concerning his salvation, these early years left doubt in their wake. On November 6, 1724, he wrote in his diary: "Felt sensibly, somewhat of that trust and affiance, in Christ, and with delight committing of my soul to him, of which our divines used to speak, and about which, I have been somewhat in doubt."

Pride and doubt were not his only antagonists during this time. Another problem emerged pertaining to the morphology of the conversion experience. On May 25, 1723, he wrote in his diary that he would diligently "look into the opinions of our old divines, concerning conversion," for, as he noted in an entry for August 12 of the same year: "The chief thing, that now makes me in any measure to question my good estate, is my not having experienced conversion in those particular steps, wherein the people of New England, and anciently the dissenters of Old England, used to experience it. Wherefore, now resolved, never to leave searching,

[9] Dwight, *Life of Edwards*, p. 151.

till I have satisfyingly found out the very bottom and foundation, the real reason, why they used to be converted in those steps." Nearly two years later he remarked: "It seems to me, that whether I am now converted or not, I am so settled in the state I am in, that I shall go on in it all my life. But, however settled I may be, yet I will continue to pray to God, not to suffer me to be deceived about it . . . and ever and anon, will call all into question and try myself, using for helps, some of our old divines." Was he converted? Why did his spiritual experiences seem to differ from the more traditional examples? Such questions form the inner fiber of Edwards' work throughout his life. He had determined "never to leave searching" until he penetrated the secret not only of his own spiritual state but of the conversion process as well. For him, as for any proper Puritan, salvation was the most important aim in his life. Without saving grace life on earth was meaningless; with it daily existence was metamorphosed into a means to heaven.

This early concern over his own spiritual state was certainly a major factor in Jonathan's increasing interest in the psychology of the human mind. On February 12, 1725, he wrote: "The very thing that I now want . . . is as clear a knowledge of the manner of God's exerting himself, with respect to Spirits and Mind, as I have, of his operations concerning Matter and Bodies." Evidently his early perception of God in terms of nature, even in terms of existence in general, proved unsatisfactory. Perhaps he realized or at least intuitively felt that such an approach reduced his mind's eye to the role of a mere subjective observer largely alienated from a distant objective God communicating through the externals of nature. In such a position the estranged self lacks true identity and, so deprived, is prone to flail about in aimless rebellion—his trouble with pride was clearly indicative. If, on the other hand, he could penetrate to some degree, however small, the mystery of his own uncertain spiritual status, if he could espy something of God's handiwork within man's inner being, then the self's impression of its remoteness from its Creator might be lessened. Eventually, after years of introspection and his role in the Great Awakening, Jonathan would realize fully the implications of his early idealism, especially of his remark in "The Mind" that "Within and Without, are mere mental conceptions."

There is one other accent in the diary deserving attention. In several of the passages from this work quoted above, Jonathan places his study of conversion in the context of how "the people of New England, and anciently the dissenters of Old England, used to experience it," of how "our divines used to speak" of it. He determines, moreover, to use "for helps, some of our old divines," writings by such men as Thomas Shepard. Particularly noteworthy in these remarks is his leaning toward tradition and orthodoxy, a disposition which should be considered as much a consequential influence on his later thought as was his early interest in Locke and Newton. Although during his undergraduate years at Yale he found himself in the midst of student unrest, there is, according to Sereno Dwight, no evidence—other than his temporary removal to Wethersfield—that he participated in these difficulties.[10] While at college Jonathan may have intellectually rebelled "against the philosophical roots of the educational system to which he was exposed," as Leon Howard has convincingly suggested,[11] but there is no reason to suppose that he ever, even then, reacted against the authority of New England Puritan tradition regarding theological matters. As his future writings make clear, orthodoxy forms the core of his thinking. Although he would find it necessary to interpret established doctrines, he always saw himself working within Puritan tradition. To rebel against orthodoxy would be to alienate an already prideful will still further from God, who communicates through the continuity of tradition as much as He does through nature. Edwards' esteem for tradition will influence the development of his notion of God's relation to the individual mind and thus will contribute importantly to his quest for selfhood, for genuine identity as a saint.

[10] Ibid., p. 29. In 1722 several members of the college, including the rector, openly embraced Episcopacy.

[11] "The Creative Imagination of a College Rebel," p. 56.

[2]

Reason and Intuition: Early Sermons

In 1727 Edwards completed his second year as tutor at Yale and accepted the post of assistant to his grandfather, the Reverend Solomon Stoddard of Northampton. Although in 1728 he preached a sermon entitled "The Excellency of Christ" which proved quite popular—"I had been earnestly importuned for a copy of it for the press," he later explained[1]—his first major work appeared in 1731, two years after Solomon Stoddard's death, when he delivered in Boston a sermon which was to become his first publication: *God Glorified in the Work of Redemption, by the Greatness of Man's Dependence upon Him in the Whole of It.* Between 1733 and 1735 Northampton underwent a religious revival or, as Edwards expressed it, a time "of extraordinary effusion of God's Spirit."[2] Although the town had been subject to several such revivals during the years under Stoddard's pastorate, this event particularly moved the youth of the community. The insecurity of their lives is, for instance, the focus of "Pressing into the Kingdom of God," a sermon Edwards delivered during this time in which he reminds his audience of "the repeated deaths of young persons amongst us."

With the revival several heretical notions resurfaced regarding man's ability to do something on his own initiative toward achieving salvation. These ideas had reared their heads time and

---

[1] "Preface," *Discourses on Various Important Subjects, Nearly Concerning the Great Affair of the Soul's Eternal Salvation,* in *Works* (Dwight), 5:350.

[2] "Pressing into the Kingdom of God," *Works* (Dwight), 5:474. The following two quotations are also from this sermon (5:476, 473).

again in New England, but Edwards witnessed the alarming extension of their sway during the revival. Consequently, in 1734, he
preached a number of sermons on the subject, the most significant
of which were "Justification by Faith Alone" and "The Justice of
God in the Damnation of Sinners." In spite of the effectiveness of
these efforts, the heresies remained unchecked, and, to make matters worse, the aroused religious affections of his parishioners inevitably waned. Edwards had forecast this decline in "Pressing into
the Kingdom of God": "Some will soon lose the sense of things they
now have; though their awakenings seem to be very considerable
for the present, they will not hold; they have not hearts disposed
to hold on through very many difficulties." The extent of this spiritual regression may in fact have surpassed his expectations; nevertheless, the wake of the revival only added impetus to Edwards'
investigation of the morphology of conversion and the inner self of
the saint.

I. *The Awful Distance*

In many respects "The Excellency of Christ" is a typical Puritan sermon. It evinces a clear sense of organization and symmetry,
which made it easy for parishioners to understand and, perhaps, to
outline. It conforms to the traditional pattern of the sermon: (1)
the identification of a biblical source, (2) the explication of the
text, (3) the presentation of doctrine and exposition, and (4) the
application or "use" of the doctrine.[3] Based on Rev. 5:5–6, Edwards' discourse presents the seeming paradox that Christ may be
characterized as both a lion and a lamb. In developing these two
polarities, Edwards constructs a chain of associations, so that
Christ's union of the qualities of these two animals typifies His
integration of glory and humility, majesty and meekness, equality
with God and reverence toward God, dominance and obedience,
sovereignty and resignation. Furthermore, the lion typifies God as
judge and the lamb represents God's creatures—both are joined in
Christ. Although not distinctive in its content, this sermon does
testify to Edwards' concern with structure and, as we shall see,
with language and style.

[3] Josephine K. Piercy, *Studies in Literary Types in Seventeenth Century
America (1607–1710)*, pp. 155–156.

Despite its reference to Christ's union of Godhead and manhood, "The Excellency of Christ" fails in general to extend much comfort to the listener. Unlike, say, the sermons on Christ delivered by Edward Taylor, this work hardly urges man to feel uplifted and encouraged by the dignity the Incarnation bestows on his earthly life. Instead it frequently stresses "the great distance" between God and man,[4] less to impress the wonder of the Incarnation upon the hearer than to humble him, to reduce his sense of self-worth. The phrase "great distance" becomes a near refrain in the sermon, reinforced by remarks that "great men" are merely "bigger worms" and God is "infinitely high above you." Man is helpless with respect to the divine Will, of which he is also miserably ignorant. God "rules over the whole universe and doth whatsoever pleaseth him"; His "decrees of future events are sealed, and shut up from all possibility of being discovered by creatures, till God is pleased to make them known." In a sermon written in June, 1735, entitled "The Sole Consideration, That God is God, Sufficient to Still All Objections to His Sovereignty," Edwards similarly declares that the "consideration alone of the infinite distance between God and us, and between God's understanding and ours, should be enough to still and quiet us concerning all that God does, however mysterious and unintelligible to us."[5]

In the concluding part or application of "The Excellency of Christ," Edwards somewhat soothes the feeling of insecurity aroused in his audience. Here he speaks of Christ as instrumental in narrowing the gap between God and man: "This is one end of Christ's taking upon him man's nature, that his people might be under advantages for a more familiar converse with him, than the infinite distance of the divine nature would allow of." The elect become like the disciples, whom Christ did not keep "at an awful distance; but all along conversed with them with the most friendly familiarity, as a father amongst a company of children." Herein lies an image of hope: "Any one of you that is a father or mother, will not despise one of your own children that comes to you in distress; much less danger is there of Christ despising you, if you in your heart come to him." Such consolation, however, is limited to

---

4 This sermon appears in *Works* (Austin), 7:267–307.
5 *Works* (Dwight), 6:296.

the elect, the adopted children of God. Just who they are remains part of the mystery of the divine Will undisclosed to man. Thus Edwards' intimations of hope are not designed to abolish altogether the feeling of insecurity generated by the earlier part of the sermon. On the contrary, they underscore the fact that instead of becoming the fortunate children of a compassionate God, most men exist "in a state of exceeding great misery." Each unregenerate person is "a poor weak creature, like an infant, cast out in its blood, in the day that it is born." Indeed, most of Edwards' audience must have felt the sting of the initial sections of this sermon only to have their mental anguish increased through the sense of desperation nurtured by the seemingly mollifying promise of the last part.

Buttressing this impression of man's estrangement from God is Edwards' repudiation of human rational powers. If man is alienated from the very source of his being by a great distance and if he is totally dependent on an arbitrary and secret divine Will, what real help can reason offer in his search for inner identity? Edwards wrote, "Our understandings, if we stretch them never so far, cannot reach up to his divine glory." Man cannot even comprehend what the distance between him and God means because he can never know that from which he is separated. Edwards' attack on the understanding—by which he meant the composite of all of the mind's rational powers—should not be read out of context. Its limitations notwithstanding, it is a precious faculty; in fact, he explained elsewhere, the understanding is the principal faculty by which God has distinguished man from the rest of creation. It is a fundamental component of the natural image of God which men bear within them, whereby they are "akin to angels, and are capable even of knowing God, of contemplating the divine Being, and his glorious perfections, manifested in his works and in his word."[6]

But even this remark, drawn from a later sermon when Edwards' understanding of the inner self would play a more significant role in narrowing the distance he early perceived between God and man, is finally restrained. Edwards would withhold any further argument for the value of human understanding, for he was well aware of the rising trend among certain of his contemporaries to regard the faculty too highly. Thus, in spite of his own

[6] "Wicked Men Useful in Their Destruction Only," *Works* (Austin), 8:146.

respect for man's rational capacities, he always maintained: "Of so little avail is human strength, or human reason and learning, as a remedy against the extreme blindness of the human mind. The blindness of the mind, or an inclination to delusion in things of religion, is so strong, that it will overcome the greatest learning, and the strongest natural reason."[7] A man of his time, Edwards allowed that we may be able to learn much about the world in which we live, but as a spokesman for Puritan tradition he clung to the belief that our knowledge of the "things of religion"—knowledge attributable not to the empirical investigations of "natural reason" but to spiritual intuition—will always remain deficient, in spite of scriptural revelation, while we dwell in this world. Only the latter sort of wisdom can end the self's search for identity.

In "The Excellency of Christ," then, Edwards assails any sense of security based on reason alone. He undercuts rational comfort not only explicitly but also implicitly in the language and style of the sermon. An early paragraph from the first part of the discourse, in which he is speaking of Christ, offers a good example of his technique:

> He is higher than the kings of the earth: For he is King of kings and Lord of lords. He is higher than the heavens, and higher than the highest angels of heaven. So great is he, that all men, all kings and princes, are as worms of the dust before him; all nations are as the drop of the bucket, and the light dust of the balance; yea, the angels themselves are as nothing before him. He is so high, that he is infinitely above any need of us; above our reach, that we cannot be profitable to him; and above our conceptions, that we cannot comprehend him.

Every phrase in this passage is carefully wrought. Each contributes in a progressive way to the eventual total realization that we cannot comprehend God. The images, it should be noted, initially ascend. The reader's mind is directed from the earthly realm of kings and lords, through the sky or heavens, to the realm of the angels. At this point the mind instinctively anticipates the next— we might say *logical*—step, namely now to pass on from angels to encounter something about God. But this rational expectation is

[7] "Man's Natural Blindness in the Things of Religion," *Works* (Dwight), 7:14.

frustrated, and the reader finds his thoughts suddenly thrust back to earth again, this time focusing on worms and dust. The immediate result of Edwards' management of language in this passage is an emotional or felt cognizance of our rational inability to comprehend God, an intuitive awareness reinforcing the explicit conclusion perceived by the conscious mind. The language of this passage is thoroughly appropriate to its content in that it too argues Edwards' point: the distance between God and man is indeed great, so vast that at best we can have only a fleeting experience or sense of Him in the affections of the heart. It is to the emotional level of the affections that the images of the passage finally appeal.

Edwards uses a second movement of images in the passage under discussion in order to underscore human ignorance and inadequacy. The series of images in this section recapitulates that of the first. Our attention is guided from kings and princes, to nations, to angels, and again its progress upward is abortive as we are left with the concept of "nothing." Yet, whereas the first sequence lacked any sort of resolution, abruptly returning to earth and beginning again, the second series does reach a climax. The resolution lies in the similes attached to the ascending images. Kings are likened to worms, nations to dust, and angels to nothing. Such a correlation frustrates the mind, for as each image in the second series ascends, its counterpart descends. Resolution is provided by cancelling the very terms of the statement. Reason thus balks, baffled by the paradox, and the reader realizes, at a felt, emotional level, what it means to be unable to come to terms with God, who is always "above our reach," beyond "our conceptions."

Now, too, the reader genuinely experiences the paradox of Christ's incorporation of the qualities of the lion and the lamb, how "there do meet in Jesus Christ infinite highness and infinite condescension." Edwards sought to thwart whatever sense of security men derived from their rational faculties and to communicate this to them explicitly, but also, more significantly, at the level of immediate intuition. No longer anchored on the ground of reason, they were to find themselves at sea emotionally. Cut adrift from the comforts of rationalizing about God's mercy, they were to confront the underlying currents of fear deep within the self. The fate of each of them, whether he was destined for salvation or for damnation, would remain unknown to him; what he could come to know was how helpless he was to save himself. Edwards wanted his audience to feel penetratingly, perhaps for the first time, that Christ's "majesty is infinitely awful."

Although the application section of this sermon allays somewhat the feelings aroused by the earlier parts, the accent of the discourse—certainly during its most forceful moments—falls on the great distance between God and man. Remoteness implies, in Edwards' view, estrangement, and, as long as one is not at peace with God, he cannot be at peace with himself. His alienation from God means that he lives in tension with a fundamental and innate inclination at the core of the self: "there is an inclination in the creature, not only to the adoration of a Lord and Sovereign, but to complacence in some one as a friend, to love and delight in some one that may be conversed with as a companion." This inherent predisposition of the self leads one to God, as the saint discovers. This tendency exists as well in the unregenerate man, indicating— were he but able to realize it—that his dissociation from the reality behind all things explains why he is alienated from himself, why he seems forever in a quandary about his selfhood.

II. *A Kind of Effusion*

On July 8, 1731, Edwards delivered the sermon *God Glorified in the Work of Redemption*, which was printed the same year. As the successor of Stoddard, who had died more than two years earlier, Edwards found himself the subject of curiosity among other divines. As the time neared for his appearance in Boston before many of them, he must have considered and reconsidered every phrase in this sermon. As a result it is one of his most tightly organized and closely reasoned works, one nearly devoid of imagery. Its intensity and rigidity intimate a self-consciousness, a self-imposed restraint on the part of the author, differentiating it from the sort of verbal brilliance evident in "The Excellency of Christ." Nevertheless, *God Glorified* was decisive in launching Edwards' career.

A cardinal tenet of Christian theology, the Trinity, provides the underlying structure for the discourse. This tripartite design is an outgrowth of the doctrine, as expressed in the sermon, that God "is the Redeemer, and the price; and . . . also is the good purchased. So that all we have is of God, and through him, and in him."[8] The prepositions *of, through,* and *in* refer to the Father, Son, and Holy Spirit respectively. The Father is the Creator, the Son the agent or means of this divine communication (Logos), and the Holy Spirit the medium of love or grace communicated. The theme emerging from this trinitarian structure focuses on the divine Will. Mankind is, Edwards declares, "dependent on God's arbitrary and sovereign good pleasure," and the recognition of God's sovereignty should underscore man's sense of distance from Him. "God is infinitely above us"; as "the great author" or "first cause" of our redemption (Father), as "the medium of it" (Son), and as goodness itself (Holy Spirit), He incorporates the ultimate reality, manifested in His Will, lying beyond the sphere of human comprehension.

This emphasis on the sovereignty of the divine Will is pertinent to Edwards' inquiry into the nature of the human self. In the sense that *God Glorified* betokens in part a response to Edwards' resolve "never to leave searching" about the experience of conversion, it represents a facet of his spiritual autobiography. Of particular importance is his investigation of the relation between the human self and the divine Self. A man's self or heart remains an enemy of God, Edwards remarks, as long as it adheres to "a selfdependent, and selfrighteous disposition." To regard the will as self-determining, as independent, is to give vent to pride, and pride is the chief of sins. In his postlapsarian state "man is naturally exceeding prone to be exalting himself and depending on his own power or goodness, as though he were he from whom he must expect happiness." This posture of self-sufficiency in actuality amounts to nothing; it constitutes a self-deception barely masking the fact that those who act in accord with this delusion are "alien from God and his Spirit."

In order to arrive at a proper notion of selfhood, man must first disabuse himself of such egocentric figments of the imagination and then turn wholly to God: "man should be emptied of himself, . . . be sensible that he is 'wretched, and miserable, and poor, and blind, and naked.' Humility is a great ingredient of true

---

[8] Quotations from this sermon are from *Works* (Austin), 7:467–485.

faith: He that truly receives redemption, receives it as a little child." Edwards, of course, has the authority of Scripture behind his association of the heart with a child. But he saw in the motif a special relevancy in that the child's self-image is yet unformed and in developing takes its character principally from parental example. This is also true for the saint, whose regenerated self stems from conformity to God with whom it identifies. Since for him God furnishes, in His trinitarian totality, the only touchstone of reality, the saint strives "to exalt God alone."

This conversion of the self depends, in its initial stage, totally upon God's voluntary communication of grace to the soul: "all the holiness and happiness of the redeemed is in God. It is in the communications, indwelling, and acting of the Spirit of God." Little is said in *God Glorified* about the specific effects of this communication; at this stage of his thought Edwards was more interested in defining the erroneous conception of selfhood. Nevertheless, this idea of the divine act of communication would eventually move from the periphery to the center of his attention and inform his later view of the saint's obligation to try to decipher the language of God. Moreover, Edwards' later investigations of the self as the recipient of this divine expression, as a secondary agent of the divine Will, would enable him to span the distance he initially thought existed between God and man. As he remarked in *God Glorified*, the Spirit dwells *within* the heart of the elect.

About midway in this sermon Edwards introduces an image which he will use with increasing frequency to portray God's influence on the self: "The saints are beautiful and blessed by a communication of God's holiness and joy, as the moon and planets are bright by the sun's light." Again, three years later in a thanksgiving sermon delivered on November 7, 1734, he would write: "Now the saints see the glory of God but by a reflected light, as we in the night see the light of the sun reflected from the moon."[9] The saintly identity or self, in other words, becomes a luminary body reflecting the enlightenment with which God favors it. "The saint," Edwards continues in *God Glorified*, "hath spiritual joy and pleasure by a kind of effusion of God on the soul. In these things the redeemed have communion with God; that is, they partake with

[9] *Works* (Dwight), 8:308.

him and of him." The direction of Edwards' thought is clear. If the principal faculty of the rational soul (the will or self) functions like a luminary, if the spiritual light it reflects in some manner joins it to God, then surely a way to read God's communication is to scrutinize that illuminated self.

Whereas in his youth Edwards discerned the divine Will in the reflections of external nature, he will more and more define it in terms of the internal autobiography of the self. That he resorts to nature for his analogy in the Boston sermon is indicative of his unconscious construction of a bridge between his youthful attachment to nature and his unfolding perception of inner identity. The analogy focuses on saintly identity or selfhood, not on nature. He sees natural phenomena as a source of types for the inner realm; he internalizes nature, employing its imagery to portray a psychic landscape. The pertinent implication of Edwards' use of nature in this fashion is the elimination of the saint's external being as any definitive basis for identity. Genuine selfhood depends on what the saint can discern and interpret of the light of divine grace communicated to his soul. This and related matters become amplified in Edwards' later writings.

God Glorified apparently received a mixed reaction from the attending divines. By 1731 many parishioners and a considerable number of ministers had begun to think that perhaps, after all, they were not quite as helpless as the religion of the earlier Puritans would have had them believe, that the performance of good works was not without some spiritual merit. By reaffirming the older notion of God's arbitrary Will, Edwards confronted this trend directly and thereby, in accord with his early penchant for the teachings of older divines, announced himself a defender of Puritan orthodoxy.

Those who hold this belief, Edwards explains in the sermon, "own that we depend on God for the gift and acceptance of a Redeemer, but deny so absolute a dependence on him for the obtaining of an interest in the Redeemer." Applying the trinitarian doctrine on which he has structured the sermon and on which he knows his listeners agree despite differences on other issues, he subtly adds that those with whom he disagrees "own an absolute dependence on the Father for giving his Son, and on the Son for working out redemption," but finally contradict themselves by failing to acknowledge "so entire a dependence on the Holy Ghost for conversion." Here Edwards adumbrates that acute alertness of mind which will characterize his mature works. Those of his audience who were impressed by the sermon saw what he had done in basing his argument on the concept that the three persons in the Trinity are inseparably united and that to limit the efficacy of one is to limit it for the other two. If any person recognizes his total dependence on the Father and on the Son, he must, in order to be consistent and nonheretical, also concede in his absolute dependence on the Holy Spirit. Since the Spirit is the dispenser of grace, as Christian thinkers all agreed, then in his dependence upon the Trinity man is helpless to merit the bestowal of the gift of the Holy Ghost. In short, if one says he is only partially dependent upon the Holy Spirit, then it follows that he likewise claims some degree of exemption from the absolute sovereignty of the Father and the Son. Edwards simply trapped his opponents and would, increasingly, rely on the continuity of Puritan tradition.

III. *An Image of Glory Beheld*

In 1734 Edwards published *A Divine and Supernatural Light, Immediately Imparted to the Soul by the Spirit of God*, a sermon marking significant refinements in his thought. In this work God is again presented as an absolute sovereign, but the enigma of an arbitrary divine Will is less in focus, and Edwards centers his discussion on the psychology of conversion. In this discourse, the predictable successor of *God Glorified*, he attempts to define more precisely what he meant by the phrase "a kind of effusion" in the Boston sermon. The conversion experience was very much on his mind at this time. The religious revival underway in his parish must have made him even more keenly concerned over his own spiritual condition. Indeed, his public writings during this time contain personal elements. It would not, for instance, be mistaken to see an intimation of his own inner unrest in a sermon, delivered in September, 1733, and entitled "The True Christian's Life, a Journey towards Heaven," in which he had suggested that "all those that are converted, are not sure of it; and those who are sure of it, do not know that they shall be always so."[10]

[10] *Works* (Austin), 7:223.

A Divine and Supernatural Light is a model of rhetorical organization. Edwards begins by discussing what is not meant by the supernatural light concomitant with conversion. It is not an acquisition of any new ideas which are not already in the Bible, nor is it necessarily "every affecting view that men have of the things of religion."[11] It does not "consist in any impression made upon the imagination." These assertions were no doubt intended to counter certain extreme positions resulting from the revival; they were personal as well, however, for Edwards' spiritual experience was extremely mild in comparison with what he was witnessing in many of his parishioners. He knew, nevertheless, that God's Will operates in ways obscure to man. Thus, since people sometimes do have such experiences, he allowed for the possibility. Although one cannot be certain that the devil is not the source of "lively impressions" on the imagination, he conceded, it is true that "when the mind has a lively discovery of spiritual things, and is greatly affected by the power of divine light, it may, and probably very commonly doth, much affect the imagination."

Equally important, the possession of supernatural light is not to be interpreted as the mere conviction of the evil of sin. Conviction of conscience is available to "natural men" as a result of "common grace," which aids the normal inclinations of the mind: "common grace only assists the faculties of the soul to do that more fully which they do by nature, as natural conscience or reason will, by mere nature make a man sensible of guilt, and will accuse and condemn him when he has done amiss." The idea expressed in this remark is a traditional one in New England Puritan thought. Regardless of whether or not the divines of the first and second generation designated the enlightenment of reason as the initial stage in conversion—there was some controversy on this point—they nevertheless concurred, at least in theory, that the illumination of this faculty alone is insufficient. Most argued that the genuine enlightenment of the understanding technically preceded the turning of the heart, the crucial stage. However, they radically differed as to the time lapse between the two and with regard to the question of whether or not this illumination preceded or followed the recep-

11 This sermon appears in ibid., 8:290–312.

tion of saving grace. The impression one receives from reading earlier divines on this subject is that analytic discourse necessarily led even those who argued for the nearly simultaneous motion of the faculties to speak *as if* they functioned somewhat independently of each other. The precise role of reason in the drama of conversion always remained for the Puritans a ticklish problem, one especially pronounced in Edwards' time.

Edwards' personal concern over his failure to experience the stages of conversion described by some of the older divines influenced his point of view in *A Divine and Supernatural Light*. In his notebook Edwards clearly indicates his belief that normally a sequence exists between reason, conscience, and the will:

> This with me is established, that grace and the exercise of grace is given entirely by the Spirit of God by His free and most arbitrary motions; but that His ordinary method, notwithstanding, is to give grace to those that are much concerned about it, and earnestly and for a considerable time seek it or continue to do things in order to it. That is, 'tis the Spirit's ordinary method first to make them concerned about it so as to convince them that 'tis best to seek it, so far as to make them seek it much, and then to bestow it. . . . So that there is doubtless in God's ordinary way a preparatory conviction of sin. . . . For God makes use of those things, viz., good nature, a good understanding, a rational brain.[12]

Yet, although God is methodical, this sequence is not delimiting, and such preparatory stages may be less dramatic or distinct, indeed almost imperceptible to the convert. Sometimes, Edwards allowed, "God, if he pleases, can convince men without such endeavours of their own . . . as must be the case in many sudden conversions."[13] Edwards not only wanted to explain some of the experiences he was witnessing during the revival at Northampton and to account for his own failure to conform to the preparatory sequence delineated by many of the older divines, but he also sought to counter any notion of man's ability to do something on his own toward his salvation. Indeed, he would later observe of his congregation in Northampton: "Particularly it was too much their

---

[12] *The Philosophy of Jonathan Edwards*, ed. Harvey G. Townsend, pp. 109–110; see also *Works* (Dwight), 8:320–354.

[13] Untitled sermon on Hos. 5:15, in *Works* (Dwight), 8:59.

method to lay almost all the stress of their hopes on the particular
steps and method of their first work, i.e. the first work of the Spirit
of God on their hearts in their convictions and conversion."[14]

Thus, in *A Divine and Supernatural Light*, he agrees that
"God, in letting in this light into the soul, deals with man according to his nature, or as a rational creature; and makes use of his
human faculties." The understanding is engaged in the drama of
conversion since it provides the means whereby one arrives at "a
notion of those doctrines that are the subject matter of this divine
light [or knowledge]; and reason may many ways be indirectly
and remotely an advantage to it." Edwards emphasizes, however,
how indirect and remote the action of this faculty is in comparison
with the turning of the heart: "if we take reason strictly, not for
the faculty of mental perception in general, but for ratiocination,
or a power of inferring by arguments . . . the perceiving of spiritual
beauty and excellency no more belongs to reason, than it belongs
to the sense of feeling to perceive colors, or to the power of seeing to
perceive the sweetness of food." Furthermore, the enlightenment
of reason does not necessarily precede but may be simultaneous
with or, in some instances, even follow the reception of grace in the
heart. Edwards never abandons the traditional claim for the importance of reason in the overall experience, but he is more than
willing to modify any focus on the illumination of this faculty
through preparatory stages, an emphasis which in his opinion too
often implies its separate character and its primacy in conversion.
He is certain that, whether or not preparatory stages are in some
way involved, "reason has also to do in the acts that are immediately consequent on this discovery: A seeing the truth of religion
from hence, is by reason; though it be by one step, and the infer-
ence be immediate." The will, of course, is finally the true locus of
supernatural light.

In making these observations Edwards differentiates between
"having an opinion, that God is holy and gracious, and having a
sense of the loveliness and beauty of that holiness and grace." The
former is merely speculative or notional knowledge, stemming
from common grace whereby the Spirit acts "upon the mind of a

---

[14] Edwards to the Reverend Thomas Gillespie, July 1, 1751, printed in Edwards, *The Great Awakening*, ed. C. C. Goen, p. 564.

natural man"; the latter is the issue of special grace whereby the Spirit "acts in the mind of a saint as an indwelling vital principle" and imparts "a new spiritual principle of life and action." Once the heart has been thus affected, then reason—if it has not already been simultaneously involved, as would most probably be the case —sincerely responds.

An important factor in Edwards' thought is the immediacy of the infusion of divine light or grace: "He imparts this knowledge immediately, not making use of any intermediate natural causes, as he does in other knowledge."[15] More intuitive than rational— except in a sense hinted at in this sermon and later defined in *A Treatise Concerning Religious Affections*—this divine light consists of "the most excellent knowledge of the angels, yea, of God himself." In fact something of Adam's original wisdom is regained, something of that internal excellency or image of God whereby he knew intuitively from the first the name or identity of everything. With special grace certain "principles are restored that were utterly destroyed by the fall."

This doctrine of immediacy is related to the diminishing importance of nature in Edwards' thinking. From the Puritan perspective, nature is rational in design and operation. According to Puritan convention, the law of reason and the law of nature are one and the same. In his younger years, as we have seen, Edwards was fascinated by the glimpses of the divine Will he discerned in nature, but even then his appreciation was not devoid of a sense of the limits of human reason in discerning nature's revelation. Reason may, as Locke argued, depend on sensual perceptions of nature (among other external things) and recollection, but for Edwards this mode of apprehending God, even though supported by Scripture, proved inadequate. In *A Divine and Supernatural Light*, he denied that the interaction of the understanding and nature offers the best source, after the Bible, for clues to the divine Will: "Men have a great deal of pleasure in human knowledge, in studies of natural things; but this is nothing to that joy which arises from this divine light shining into the soul." The best place, it follows, to search for an expression of divine intent is the human heart, not in

[15] Edwards' doctrine of immediacy is excellently discussed in Douglas J. Elwood, *The Philosophical Theology of Jonathan Edwards.*

nature (as many of his deistic contemporaries were inclined to think). The light of grace reflected in the heart of the saint is *super*natural; the saint, Edwards remarked a year earlier in "The True Christian's Life, a Journey towards Heaven," will take "a transient view" of pleasant places, flowery meadows, or shady groves."[16] To be sure, Edwards never dismissed reason or nature as useless; rather, he sought to put them into perspective. Thus his idealism gradually supplanted his empiricism. For him reality (i.e., God) is less vitally encountered through reason's postlapsarian responses to nature than through an impression which the Spirit makes on the heart. The human will or self became for him a clearer index than nature to the divine Will.

Looked at superficially, *A Divine and Supernatural Light* might paradoxically seem a very rational sermon about the limits of reason. The fact is, however, that underlying its formal structure and argumentation is a management of language similar in effect to that in "The Excellency of Christ." Edwards' language in this sermon communicates a feeling or sense of its ideas. At the simplest level Edwards reiterates a few conventional images, as for instance when he speaks of "the dawning of the light of glory in the heart" that gives "the mind peace and brightness in this stormy and dark world." He may have meant his audience to recall how they feel each dawn as the influx of life's energy returns to the gradually awakening body; possibly he intended them to reexperience in their mind the sense of relief and renewal that comes with the dawn following a dark, stormy night. The latter image certainly was pertinent to Edwards, for as a child he was terrified by thunder and lightning. After his own internal dawn—whether or not it was a genuine rebirth was the nagging question—these phenomena became precious to him. The way in which such images or natural types were meant to work artistically is, I think, suggested in the following passage from the sermon: "There is a difference between having a rational judgment that honey is sweet, and having a sense of its sweetness. A man may have the former, that knows not how honey tastes; but a man cannot have the latter unless he has an idea of the taste of honey in his mind." No words can describe the taste of honey; each member of the audience must

16 *Works* (Austin), 7:210.

supply the context if he is to experience the meaning of the comment. It is precisely this moment of experienced or felt thought that Edwards aims for in his artistry. The attempt to elicit such inner sensations informs, we might say, the stylistic principle of decorum operative in many of his early sermons. He wishes to convey to his audience, at an emotional level, what is meant by the "inward sweetness" of grace.

Edwards recognized that images always threatened to get out of hand and might finally distract more than instruct. This is most likely why *A Divine and Supernatural Light* lacks the sort of imagery found in, say, "Jesus Christ Gloriously Exalted." Nevertheless, Edwards' principle of decorum still functions in this work with regard to style. The sentences of this discourse are declarative rather than hortatory, each projecting its meaning forward incisively. Nearly every phrase seems constructed so that its stress is not obscured by the flow of words. Edwards intensifies the effect of this technique by fashioning repeated phrases which become, in a sense, formulaic devices. In one paragraph, for example, he uses the phrase "there is a difference" twice, then adds a little more emphasis in "so there is a difference," concluding with "there is a wide difference." The outcome of such a slowly expanding formula is twofold: it lends a concreteness, a heavy seriousness, to the ideas it introduces and it tends to contribute an emotional dimension to our apprehension of the thoughts. Effective repetition of this sort becomes incantatory, somewhat hypnotic, finally communicating to an audience, at the level of feeling, a dimension which cannot, any more than it could with regard to the image of honey, be attained by mere rational comprehension.

Rhetorical control is similarly demonstrated in the conclusion of the sermon. Noting that "it is rational to suppose, that it should be beyond a man's power to obtain this knowledge and light by the mere strength of natural reason," Edwards closes the sermon by referring to four points progressively more difficult for the human mind to comprehend. He repeats first of all the simple difference between speculative knowledge and divine light; next, he contrasts secular joy with spiritual sweetness; third, he speaks of the effects of this light on the soul; and last, he refers to a "universal holiness of life," a "universal obedience" originating from "a sincere love to

God, which is the only principle of a true, gracious, and universal obedience." In effect, this expanding definition progresses from the external world to the inner self. The ultimate context, the reality of God, lies within the self of the saint; with supernatural light he intuitively knows what is true and good, and, consequently, he does not require any external frame of reference provided by the world in which he lives. Special grace "assimilates the nature [of the soul] to the divine nature, and changes the soul into an image of the same glory that is beheld." This idea is what Edwards has in mind whenever he speaks of the soul as a luminary mirroring divine light. The inner self or heart becomes for him more revelatory of the divine Will than does nature.

When we consider how the ideas and techniques of many of Edwards' early sermons emphasize the inward sensation of grace as opposed to an intellectual response, we understand better why his parishioners, encouraged by their pastor, were enjoying a religious revival in Northampton. He had learned that neither a rationally governed series of steps, extended over a long period of time, nor an inflamed emotional response necessarily characterizes the drama of conversion. Generally, he concluded, the reception of grace is in fact peaceful in nature, though it always brings about, in its immediacy, a felt sensation in the heart. Edwards hoped to communicate this fact to his parishioners, not merely rationally but emotionally—as if to give them a foretaste of the experience. This is the principle of decorum functioning in the best of these early sermons: through the careful management of language and style Edwards sought to move the hearts of his audience in a way which simulated and, perhaps, prepared those same hearts for the sensation that accompanies the reception of supernatural light.

IV. *Of Fig Leaves and Nakedness*

By 1734 New England had become considerably secularized. Increased population and prosperity made the colonists less amenable to the severity of earlier Puritan dogma and laws. Many had learned that in the business of daily life one usually receives compensation in proportion to the amount of effort exerted. This in turn fostered a respect for the human will. Consequently, Arminian ideas became increasingly popular because, in contrast to the portrait of man as utterly passive and helpless before a sovereign God, they focused on man's rational faculties and on his ability to do something to merit his salvation. As a defender of early orthodoxy Edwards felt compelled to counter the rising tide of Arminian influence, and in 1734 he delivered several sermons on the subject.

In "Justification by Faith Alone" Edwards reasserts the essential doctrine he had argued in *God Glorified*: that God possesses absolute sovereignty in determining who is justified or saved. This is one of the "first principles of the Christian faith," he remarks in his introduction to the book including this sermon, and faith necessarily involves "great mysteries."[17] By referring to the mystery involved in such a fundamental doctrine, he prepares for his assault on those who overvalue human reason; for, quite simply, if something is a mystery it lies, by definition, beyond rational scrutiny. Edwards is careful, however, to temper his comments. Despite his contentions regarding its limitations, as we noted earlier, he never repudiates the role of the understanding. Thus he allows that "there is room for progress in the knowledge" of doctrinal mysteries "and doubtless will be to the end of the world." God's secret Will is progressively revealed to mankind in historical time. There exists, however, a fixed nucleus around which this advancing revelation unfolds, and for Edwards this stable center is discernible in the continuity of traditional Puritan dogma.

A person is justified, Edwards explains in the discourse, "when he is approved of God as free from the guilt of sin and its deserved punishment." Justification comes "by faith only, and not any virtue or goodness of our own."[18] Elsewhere he speaks of faith in terms identical to those he uses to describe special grace. Faith is "a sense and conviction of his [Christ's] goodness and reality as

[17] Quotations from this sermon and from "The Justice of God in the Damnation of Sinners" are from *Works* (Austin), 7:9–130, 326–374. For the "Preface," however, see *Works* (Dwight), 5:347–350.

[18] For a discussion of certain ambiguities in Edwards' treatment of this doctrine, see Conrad Cherry, *The Theology of Jonathan Edwards*, pp. 90–106, and Thomas Schafer, "Jonathan Edwards and Justification by Faith," *Church History* 20 (December 1951): 55–67.

such"; "Faith is that inward sense and act, of which prayer is the expression."[19] As with supernatural light, the sensation of faith is something men cannot merit. Edwards admonishes in "Justification by Faith Alone" that any contrary belief betokens pride and makes men rebels against God. The abandonment of this false sense of self and the total submission to divine authority, to the sensation of faith, is required if the soul which is "separate and alienated from Christ" is to be united with Him. No longer in rebellion, the humbled self encounters the reality of God, and within this source of all being it locates genuine identity. What it discovers is divine holiness and goodness (God's excellency or beauty), and the identity it achieves is a reflection of these qualities in the soul.[20] This "goodness and loveliness of the person in the acceptance of God," Edwards cautions his Arminian opponents, "in any degree, is not to be considered [as] prior but posterior in the order and method of God's proceeding in this affair." The soul can mirror divine excellency only after the proper foundation for selfhood has been established by Christ, only after the gift of faith has been bestowed upon it. Now firmly grounded on the reality of God, the will can at last act. Now Christ and the saint engage in a "mutual act" wherein "each should receive the other."[21]

"Justification by Faith Alone" was not a popular sermon. Edwards reports that he was "greatly reproached for defending this doctrine in the pulpit . . . suffering a very open abuse for it." But the laity of Northampton, as a result of his previous sermons, were ripe for an influx of religious enthusiasm. By the time he preached "The Justice of God in the Damnation of Sinners"—in his own estimation his most effective discourse—the revival had reached its apogee.

This sermon commences with a reiteration of Edwards' usual concerns: God's sovereignty, man's helplessness resulting from sin, God's justice in damning the wicked. He accents the awfulness of God's sovereignty, how it is simultaneously marvellous to ponder and terrifying to confront. Punishment, he adds, is warranted in

---

[19] *Works* (Austin), 4:437, 440.

[20] A careful, important study of the relation between religious feeling and divine beauty is Roland André Delattre's *Beauty and Sensibility in the Thought of Jonathan Edwards*.

[21] See also *Works* (Dwight), 8:307.

direct proportion to the honor of the person whom one offends, and, since God is infinitely honorable, one's transgressions against Him merit eternal damnation. Man can do nothing to alleviate this retribution. Only God, as the affronted party, can temper justice with mercy.

Those among Edwards' parishioners who were inclined to a somewhat more lenient position no doubt followed this line of reasoning without many qualms. They would have judged what he had said as true enough, but they would have derived some comfort from the idea that God's mercy was abundant, more inclusive than traditional Puritanism taught. Surely, they might have said to themselves, the religious and secular prosperity of the community indicates God's favor. Moreover, were they not living as good Christians, as well as one could reasonably expect? After all, they may have objected, "God shews mercy to others that have done these things as well as I, yea, that have done a great deal worse than I."

Prepared for such a rebuttal, Edwards directly confronts this final strand of security. He first relies on the orthodox Puritan notion that whatever one does—thought, word, deed—comprises "the language of [the] heart" or self.[22] He then proceeds to enumerate the shortcomings to which everyone is prone, if not entirely, at least to some degree: the use of profanity; the entertainment of "worldly, vain and unprofitable thoughts"; the gratification of "lusts in your imaginations"; the preference for "vain company"; the ridiculing of parents; the desire for revenge; and so forth. "How many sorts of wickedness have you been guilty of," Edwards scolds, "How manifold have been the abominations of your life?"

The indictment is incisive: if what one does represents the language of the heart, if "the will always necessarily approves of, and rests in its own acts," then these numerous imperfections reveal the sinfulness of the soul. So much for those who feel secure in living a Christian life as well as they can. What once appeared to them as minor offences becomes oppressive when viewed collectively, and the very preponderance of these failings is inescapable. Edwards' audience knew that what they *did* actually revealed more than what they *intended*. They might strive in earnest to

---

[22] See also *Works* (Austin), 8:43.

love God, but their good intentions were always undercut by the indisputable fact that their actions—daily thoughts, words, and deeds to which they hardly gave consideration at the time—betrayed them as hypocrites. Here is Edwards' empiricism used with a vengeance; how could the accused argue away these observable facts, how could anyone feel secure when seemingly minor transgressions, habitual and unconscious, plainly testified to a corrupt heart? "The blame lies at your door," Edwards indicts them; "Sew fig leaves as you will, your nakedness will appear." Stripped of devout or of frequently presumptuous intentions, human actions leave the descendents of Adam naked before God's justice as if the fall in Eden were endlessly recapitulated within the heart.

Edwards bared the self in this sermon, the self not garbed in the wedding robes of grace. The presumption engendered by pride or "selflove" has no foundation, because the demonstrable fact remains, according to Edwards, that each man is "a little, wretched, despicable creature; a worm, a mere nothing, and less than nothing; a vile insect, that has risen up in contempt against the Majesty of heaven and earth." An insect, so insignificant, so vulnerable that it might be crushed accidentally or, perhaps, deliberately without much effort—this was Edwards' image of man awaiting divine justice. His discourse was directed at rooting out the presumptuous security and self-love which he detected in the hearts of the laity and which he was personally anxious about because of his own tendency toward arrogance. He therefore used strong language in this sermon in order to evoke a sense of humility in the hearer. Humility is, finally, the theme of "The Justice of God in the Damnation of Sinners." When the heart abandons all hope in its own ability, when it no longer presumes on God's mercy, then in selfless abasement it is ready for supernatural light and genuine identity.

In our discussion of *God Glorified*, it was noted in passing that Edwards' investigation into the nature of the self and his respect for Puritan tradition are mutually inclusive concerns. This relation is equally evident in our comments on "Justification by Faith Alone" and "The Justice of God in the Damnation of Sinners." For Edwards the continuity of traditional Puritan dogma, preserved through succeeding generations, comprises a collective

self. In other words, he discerned a quintessential identity at the core of Puritanism which, he thought, remained fixed because, like the individual self of the saint, it is infused with the light of God's Will.[23] His quest for selfhood paralleled his recognition of and respect for this collective self; his inner search was, in fact, partially resolved in terms of it. His defense of orthodoxy throughout his career tended to reinforce the sense of identity he privately sought within himself. The risk was, however, that in the process he might alienate the very people he was trying to serve as a spokesman for the divine Will revealed in Puritan history and tradition.

[23] For a discussion of this idea in another context see my "Anonymity and Art in *The Life and Death of That Reverend Man of God, Mr. Richard Mather,*" *American Literature* 42 (January 1971): 457–467. Of tangential interest is Gerhard T. Alexis, "Jonathan Edwards and the Theocratic Ideal," *Church History* 35 (September 1966): 328–343.

[3]

Parents and Children:
Works of the Postrevival Period

By May, 1735, the revival had declined, and Edwards began to ponder what had occurred. A letter from Benjamin Colman of Boston requesting information about the Northampton experience provided him with a specific opportunity to examine further what he had learned about conversion. The reply to Colman was seminal, and Edwards soon undertook to rewrite his description. The resulting work, correctly entitled *A Faithful Narrative of the Surprising Work of God in the Conversion of Many Hundred Souls, in Northampton, and the Neighboring Towns and Villages of the County of Hampshire, in the Province of the Massachusetts Bay in New England*, proved to be a singularly popular book, seeing three editions and twenty printings within two years.

I. *As a Child with a Father*

The time, Edwards explains in *A Faithful Narrative*, was one of "a remarkable religious concern"; "this seems to have been a very extraordinary dispensation of Providence: God has in many respects gone out of, and much beyond his usual and ordinary way."[1] Although people of all ages were affected, Edwards is particularly cognizant of the changes in the youth of the town. By the 1730's not only was piety less evident in people generally, at least

[1] This study is printed in Edwards, *The Great Awakening*, ed. C. C. Goen, pp. 128–211.

from the point of view of many ministers, but the youth seemed the very offspring of prosperity and social self-awareness. "It was their manner," Edwards reports, "very frequently to get together in conventions of both sexes, for mirth and jollity, which they called frolics; and they would often spend the greater part of the night in them." It is on youth, from small child to young adult, that *A Faithful Narrative* focuses. Significantly, the two case studies Edwards presents in this work concern a young woman, Abigail Hutchinson, and a child four years of age, Phebe Bartlet.

The emphasis on youth in this book actually serves as a facet of Edwards' more pervasive attention to the image of the Puritan family. This image was crucial to early Puritans' view of themselves. For them the family represented a principle of order, the basic social unit, the very foundation of church and state. The fundamentals of Puritan government were initially grounded on the familial hierarchy, according to which a husband was said to be superior to his wife and both parents the respected masters of their children. Civil order, the maintenance of which was vital to fulfilling the Puritan founders' covenant with God, depended on how well this family unit was preserved. Based on readings of Scripture and on the law of nature, the system implied that the more pious and intelligent should rule over the less religious and wise. Everyone had a duty to discover and then meet the obligations of his place in this scheme, whether merely familial or more widely social. As the Puritan colonies matured, the sense of unity and the authority engendered by this ideal waned in the family, in the church, and in the town. In 1736 Edwards tried to brighten the dimming image of the Puritan family and to resuscitate the sentiment once associated with it.

Taking the family hierarchy as his point of departure in *A Faithful Narrative*—the motif was latent and undeveloped in his earlier letter version sent to Colman—Edwards points to the dereliction of parents as the key to the shortcomings of youth. He complains, simply, that "family government did too much fail in the town." Even the suicide of his Uncle Hawley, albeit not precisely the result of the deficiencies Edwards had in mind, was attributable to defects in the man's family background; he "was of a family that are exceedingly prone to the disease of melancholy."

Edwards' penchant for the traditional led him to reemphasize the image of the family unit; if he could once again breathe life into it he would be able, he thought, to reverse the trend toward secularization so evident in youth's sentiments and also to curtail the concomitant dissolution of authority. Thus, asserting the principles of family hierarchy, he "urged on heads of families, that it would be a thing agreed upon among them, to govern their families and keep their children at home." How emotional an issue this was for him becomes clear in the following passage from the sermon "Great Care Necessary, Lest We Live in Some Way of Sin":

> When parents lose their government over their children, their reproofs and counsel signify but little. How many parents are there who are exceedingly faulty on this account! How few are there who are thorough in maintaining order and government in their families! How is family government in a great measure vanished! and how many are as likely to bring a curse upon their families, as Eli! This is one principal ground of the corruptions which prevail in the land. This is the foundation of so much debauchery, and of such corrupt practices among young people. Family government is in a great measure extinct. By neglect in this particular, parents bring the guilt of their children's sins upon their own souls, and the blood of their children will be required at their hands.[2]

In *A Faithful Narrative*, the renewal of family hierarchy, unity, and harmony characterizes a fundamental consequence of the surprising work of the Holy Spirit in Northampton. The revival becomes "a time of joy in families on the account of salvation's being brought unto them; parents rejoicing over their children as newborn, and husbands over their wives, and wives over their husbands." In Edwards' portraits of Phebe and Abigail the reader sees two girls who are surrounded by their respective families, the members of which provide mutual spiritual benefit. Phebe is not only "very still and attentive at home in prayer time"—she finds herself particularly "affected in time of family prayer"—but she is also very anxious about the spiritual welfare of her sisters, on whom she is a good influence:

> The same day the elder children, when they came home from school, seemed much affected with the extraordinary change that

[2] *Works* (Austin), 8:108.

seemed to be made in Phebe: and her sister Abigail standing by, her mother took occasion to counsel her, now to improve her time, to prepare for another world: on which Phebe burst out in tears and cried out, "Poor Nabby!" Her mother told her she would not have her cry, she hoped that God would give Nabby salvation; but that did not quiet her, she continued earnestly crying for some time; and when she had in a measure ceased, her sister Eunice being by her, she burst out again and cried, "Poor Eunice!" and cried exceedingly; and when she had almost done, she went into another room, and there looked upon her sister Naomi: and burst out again, crying, "Poor Amy!"

Older than Phebe, Abigail Hutchinson represents the young adult who becomes likewise a spiritual influence on her family. Whereas, in her own opinion, she once was guilty of "want of duty to parents," she becomes an exemplary daughter during the revival. She learns, as well, that the earthly family is a shadow or type of the heavenly family, for her filial behaviour at home is reinforced by "as immediate an intercourse with [God] as a child with a father."

To be sure, both narratives admonish youth. But they equally instruct parents concerning their responsibility in governing and caring for their children. As portrayed by Edwards, Phebe's parents are wise, patient, and gentle; nevertheless, they nearly miss the signs of her conversion: "Her parents did not know of it at that time, and were not wont, in the counsels they gave to their children, particularly to direct themselves to her, by reason of her being so young, and as they supposed not capable of understanding." Phebe's parents had not been sufficiently perceptive in discerning God's work. As a result of this failure, the family hierarchy is briefly inverted, and the parents learn from their four-year-old child. Had this reversal of roles persisted, the Bartlets would have exemplified the problem Edwards had perceived in those families whose children were undisciplined. But the proper familial relationship was soon restored in the Bartlet household, and in the remainder of this part of *A Faithful Narrative* Phebe's mother emerges as a prominent figure.

In speaking of the Puritan image of the family we touched on larger religious and social implications, specifically that the well-ordered family symbolized the successful religious community. In terms of this extended ring of meaning, the minister is the spiritual father or head of the communal family. This is what Edwards meant when, speaking in *The Resort and Remedy of Those That Are Bereaved by the Death of an Eminent Minister* (a sermon on the decease of the Reverend William Williams), he remarked how "God has now taken away from you an able and faithful minister of the New Testament, one that has long been a father to you, and a father in our Israel."[3] As a defender of orthodoxy, Edwards was particularly sensitive to this image, clinging to it as the sine qua non of Puritanism at a time when such a notion was becoming increasingly unpopular and when many ministers felt they were losing control of their congregations. In *A Faithful Narrative*, therefore, he admonishes parents not only to be more attentive to their family obligations but also, in turn, to regard their own place in the larger communal family under the direction of ministerial authority. In this sense Abigail and Phebe become more than model children; they become paragons of filial devotion to their spiritual father. Abigail, Edwards tells us, "was like a little child" in her relationship with him; she "wanted to live at my house that I might tell her her duty." Phebe too sees the minister as a father-figure and responds to him as a child would to a beloved parent. She "manifested great love to her minister," according to Edwards, and, on one occasion when he had just arrived in town after a long trip, "she appeared very joyful at the news, and told the children of it, with an elevated voice, as the most joyful tidings; repeating it over and over, 'Mr. Edwards is come home! Mr. Edwards is come home!' "

These individual portraits illustrate the character of the revival in Northampton. "This work of God," Edwards recalls, "had also a good effect to unite the people's affections much to their minister"; "both old and young have shewn a forwardness to hearken not only to my counsels, but even to my reproofs from the pulpit" and "I know of no one young person in the town that has returned to former ways of looseness and extravagancy." For Edwards the reassertion of his parental role in the community provided an index, a traditional one, to God's extraordinary reaffirmation of His covenant with New England.

[3] Ibid., p. 404.

The trouble was, however, that by the time he was writing *A Faithful Narrative* the energy of the revival was already dissipating: "in the main there was a gradual decline of that general, engaged, lively spirit in religion, which had been before." Furthermore, the old tensions between the desires of the people and the authority of the clergy were soon in evidence again, most notably in the controversy over the appointment of Robert Breck by the Springfield congregation in opposition to the wishes of neighboring ministers. Edwards wrote an orthodox defense of ministerial authority in the matter after the Massachusetts General Assembly upheld the rights of the congregation and Breck was ordained.[4] Even while writing *A Faithful Narrative*, Edwards no doubt sensed that something was lost; from beneath an apparent exuberance emerges more than a hint of unconscious wistfulness in his portraits of Abigail and Phebe's affection for their spiritual father. Consciously, however, Edwards asserted his fatherly role, trying to keep alive both the traditional image and the sentiments associated with it by earlier generations of Puritans. Hopefully he and his filial parishioners would extend the ring of the communal family and, as children of God, finally be united in the family of Christ in heaven.

If the image of the family provides something of a structural motif for *A Faithful Narrative*, it also directly relates to the theme of the work, conversion. Conversion most readily occurs when the environment is appropriate, and the restoration of family order provides that environment. It struck Edwards as fitting that this period of extraordinary dispensation of grace should occur in conjunction with the renewal of the family unit (in all its ramifications), for this traditional image is particularly germane to the notion of God's special covenant with New England.

A Faithful Narrative served Edwards as an opportunity to extend his earlier inquiries into the nature of the conversion experience, and his interest in the traditional stages delineated by earlier divines enters into his discussion. Generally "persons are first awakened with a sense of their miserable condition by nature," he explains, and of these "some are more suddenly seized with con-

---

[4] *A Narrative and Defence of the Proceedings of the Ministers of Hampshire, Who Disapproved of Mr. Breck's Settlement at Springfield.*

victions . . . their consciences are suddenly smitten"; then, for the truly elect, follows the crucial turning of the heart. But Edwards does not think of this customary scheme as exclusive: "in some God makes use of their own reason much more sensibly than in others." The awakening of reason and the conviction of conscience, as we noted before, are certainly involved in the experience but not always as distinctly as earlier divines tended to think. Ultimately the precise compass of conversion remains unpredictable. From his own experience and, as well, from what he had witnessed during the Northampton revival, Edwards concluded that "the manner of God's work on the soul is (sometimes especially) very mysterious."

Nowhere in *A Faithful Narrative* does Edwards support the notion, gaining prominence at this time, that true conversion is necessarily accompanied by emotional enthusiasm. Rather, he sought to effect a balance between those who stressed reason and those who emphasized emotion in the drama of conversion. Reason and emotion are both involved, he argued, but generally in a subdued manner. Reason is clearly included—ten years later he would be much more explicit on this point—but the turning of the heart was decisive. The truly converted must "have intuitively beheld, and immediately felt, most illustrious works and powerful evidence of divinity in them." Edwards again accents intuition and immediacy; if phases or stages exist, they may be imperceptible in many instances. Yet he carefully avoids any extremist deductions from this doctrine. Qualifying his idea, he notes that this emotional element does not generate frenzy but yields "a calmness, and then the light gradually comes in; small glimpses at first."

Edwards was not only limiting the range of the enthusiast and trying to resolve the dilemma posed by his own inward experience, he was also salvaging the older view of the stages of conversion. There may often appear to be preparatory stages—God is methodical—but grace is received immediately and is not of necessity dependent upon such a priori steps. Furthermore, whereas such phases may be imperceptible in the elect before their conversion, they are certainly in evidence afterward. Generally the influx of grace in the soul is not blinding or ravishing; it tends to be a gentle sensation giving rise to progressive stages of a posteriori development. As he explained in *A Faithful Narrative*, the chosen "have a little taste of the sweetness of divine grace, and the love of a Saviour, when terror and distress of conscience begins to be turned into an humble, meek sense of their own unworthiness before God; and there is felt inwardly, perhaps, some disposition to praise God; and after a little while the light comes in more clearly and powerfully." The effect can be so calm, he cautioned, that "they have no imagination that they are now converted, it don't so much as come into their minds." Edwards had attained significant insight into the nature of conversion, especially his own experience. Indeed, from this perspective, might not his very motivation "never to leave searching" about his spiritual condition stem from the a posteriori effects of grace in his soul? He would eventually answer this question in the affirmative, when it became still clearer to him that in the saint the stages generally thought to be preparatory were in actuality already responses to the presence of grace in the soul.

The nature of the self, the stage of the drama of conversion, was very much on Edwards' mind in 1737. In an untitled sermon derived from Hos. 2:15, he asserts that postlapsarian man "naturally trusts in himself, and magnifies himself. And for man to enjoy only ease and prosperity and quietness tends to nourish and establish such a disposition."[5] Real security, genuine identity, is absent in this condition. God must first "humble the soul, before he gives true hope and comfort in conversion."

In *A Faithful Narrative* humility likewise emerges as the key to the virtuous heart. A "resignation to God, and humble submission to his will" provide the foundation for true identity of the self. The humiliated will abandons perverse willfulness for pious willingness. One must be able to say with Abigail, "I am quite willing to live, and quite willing to die; quite willing to be sick, and quite willing to be well; and quite willing for anything that God will bring upon me!" A subtle paradox lies in Abigail's voluntary passivity. Such humility actually constitutes an assertion of her faculty of will.[6] She can exercise this faculty properly because she

[5] *Works* (Dwight), 8:75, 76, 96.
[6] On active-passivity see my *The Will and the Word: The Poetry of Edward Taylor*, pp. 66–76.

possesses true identity, genuine selfhood. Her will, no longer subjectively deluded by pride, is in touch with the ultimate objective
reality of the divine Will or Self. The saint, Edwards puts the
matter succinctly, possesses "an inward firm persuasion of the
reality of divine things."

This perception of reality is *inward*. In *A Faithful Narrative*,
we again see Edwards' shift from his youthful fascination with
natural phenomena. In this work, as in *God Glorified*, images derived from nature tend to be internalized, portraying the inner
landscape of the heart where God's communication is more vitally
direct and immediate. Thus we read that grace in men ignorant of
their election is "like the trees in winter, or like seed in the spring
suppressed under a hard clod of earth." Hope will eventually
arouse their hearts "into life and vigor, as the warm beams of the
sun in the spring have quickened the seeds and productions of the
earth":

> In some, converting light is like a glorious brightness suddenly
> shining in upon a person, and all around him: they are in a re-
> markable manner brought out of darkness into marvellous light.
> In many others it has been like the dawning of the day, when at
> first but a little light appears, and it may be is presently hid with
> a cloud; and then it appears again, and shines a little brighter,
> and gradually increases, with intervening darkness, till at length,
> perhaps, it breaks forth more clearly from behind the clouds.

Edwards fails to transform his imagery into genuine metaphors in
this instance, but the implication is clear. The self remains at the
center of his discussion in this passage, and nature imagery serves
to depict a spiritual landscape. Nature, with its images or shadows
of divine things, supplies types of the inner terrain. Like nature,
the self reflects God's excellency, but it mirrors this divine communication in a more essential manner. The inner self will steadily
occupy Edwards' attention.

It may be somewhat fanciful to suggest a connection between
Edwards' notion of the self and his view of Northampton, but a
striking correspondence exists. In his opinion the isolation of
Northampton from other towns, its "being so far within the land,
at a distance from seaports," accounts for its exemption from much
of the vice manifest elsewhere. This principle of isolation is, I

think, precisely at the core of Edwards' regard for the inner region of the heart. I do not mean to imply that he is renouncing natural beauty or activity in the world; rather, he is repudiating the world as a real foundation for such perception and action. The gracious self, humbled and immediately in touch with divine reality, is isolated from the subjective deceptions it encounters in the natural world. It perceives divine reality more vitally through an inwardly felt sensation than through the deluding senses of the body. This becomes clear in another passage relating geography and the heart, written about a year later in a sermon entitled "Joseph's Great Temptation and Gracious Deliverance," in which Edwards once again finds it necessary to condemn frolicking: "I do not send you far off to find out whether the custom be not of bad tendency—not beyond the sea, to some distant country; I send you no further than to your own breast . . . [there] let the matter be determined."[7] Edwards builds his world within because the heart is the touchstone of reality; only pride, especially spiritual pride, "that grand inlet of the Devil into the hearts of men,"[8] can threaten to penetrate its insularity.

This emphasis on the integrity of the inner self parallels Edwards' fondness for the family motif; the traditional image of the family is, for him, insulated against the vicissitudes of time and place because it objectifies the collective self of Puritanism. God reveals His Will through the collective self just as He does through the individual heart of the saint. For Edwards, the private self of the saint and the collective self implied in the Puritan family are as inseparably aligned as were the spread of conversion and the revival of familial authority in Northampton.

Even as the first complete edition of *A Faithful Narrative* was being printed, the mood of the revival declined and Northampton backslid. The children, in Edwards' opinion, were again out of control. In 1738, as we just noted, he delivered a sermon attacking the behavior of youth, particularly with regard to frolicking, a "practice that leads and exposes to sin." "Joseph's Great Temptation" indicts negligent parents, who—more attuned to the liberalizing

7 *Works* (Austin), 7:131–158.
8 Edwards to the Reverend Thomas Gillespie, July 1, 1751, printed in Edwards, *The Great Awakening*, p. 563.

social trends of early eighteenth-century America than their pastor
—permitted their children to attend festivities in order that they
might learn how to conduct themselves in the company of others.
Edwards condemns the custom without hedging. Once again structuring his argument around the traditional Puritan image of the
family, he remarks that "heads of families, if they have any government over their children; or any command of their own houses,
would not tolerate their children in such practices." Yet the regen-
erating work of the Holy Spirit in Northampton families now
seemed vanquished. The confident note expressed through the family motif in *A Faithful Narrative*, albeit not without a darker undercurrent, becomes an uncertain echo in "Joseph's Great Temptation."

Moreover, when this religious fervor was declining in 1738,
Edwards personally sensed his waning authority as a spiritual
father. All he could do was bluntly declare his position: "I desire
our young people to suffer their ears to be open to what I have to
say upon this point; as I am the messenger of the Lord of Hosts to
them." This assertion is too bald, too emphatic. It unmasks Edwards' wavering sense of certitude about his previous assessment of
the Spirit's work in Northampton. It also alerts us to an increasing
awareness of his isolation from his community and it foreshadows
his downfall. Disillusioned, he will now turn to the larger context
provided by history in order to reassess his sense of mission as an
ambassador of Christ.

II. *The Grand Design*

In 1739 Edwards gave a series of discourses on the continuity
of divine Providence as disclosed by history. Although these sermons were never published during his life, he saw in them the
nucleus of a major treatise, *A History of the Work of Redemption*,
"a body of divinity in an entire new method, being thrown into the
form of a history."[9]

The work describes three periods of time. The first era, spanning four thousand years, extends from the fall of Adam to the
Incarnation. It includes five principal subdivisions: Adam and Eve

[9] Dwight, *Life of Edwards*, p. 569.

after the fall; Noah after the flood; patriarchs Abraham, Isaac, and Jacob and their special calling by God; Moses in the wilderness; and David's reign over the Jews. The second epoch is comprised of the Incarnation and the Resurrection of Christ. The final period encompasses, in phases balancing those of the first period, all history subsequent to the Resurrection: the destruction of Jerusalem, the rise of Constantine, the dominance of the Roman Catholic Church, the emergence of the Reformation, and the ultimate conquest of the Antichrist. Edwards' overall purpose in this account is to reveal the continuity of history, to indicate how every historical event contributes to one "grand design."[10]

In theological terms this design emerges from the convenant made between the Father and the Son to redeem certain men from their fallen condition. Edwards endorses the traditional Puritan understanding of this contract as an "eternal covenant of redemption which was between the Father and the Son before the foundation of the world. Every decree of God is in some way or other reducible to that covenant." This work of redemption, Edwards explains, is only virtually, not actually, completed by Christ's resurrection. Salvation occurs in terms of the total fullness of time or history: "the whole dispensation, as it includes the preparation and the purchase, and the application and success of Christ's redemption, is here called the work of redemption."

The preparation and application of Christ's work involve another contract, the covenant of grace. Only those chosen by God, for reasons He alone knows, share in this relation. The saints in no way merit their election; they remain utterly dependent upon God's arbitrary Will. If they are chosen, however, they eventually receive special grace and are destined for eternal life in heaven. The covenant of grace supersedes the covenant of works, which was in effect before the fall. The older covenant permitted Adam some power of his own in that he could maintain his Edenic existence as long as he voluntarily obeyed God's law. When he disobeyed, Adam lost this ability for himself and the rest of mankind, with the consequence that since the fall all men are completely

---

[10] No text of the *History* is satisfactory, because editors have felt compelled to improve Edwards' rough style in this work. I am quoting from *Works* (Austin), 2:9–392.

helpless spiritually. The covenant of works was abrogated, replaced by the new covenant. Both are part of the grand design Edwards perceives in history. History is the actualization of Christ's covenant of redemption.

The underlying pattern of history is so concrete for Edwards that he turns to architecture (suggested no doubt by 1 Cor. 3:10–17) for many of the images he associates with it:

> Like an house or temple that is building; first, the workmen are sent forth, then the materials are gathered, then the ground fitted, then the foundation is laid, then the superstructure is erected, one part after another, till at length the top stone is laid, and all is finished. Now the work of redemption in that large sense that has been explained, may be compared to such a building, that is carrying on from the fall of man to the end of the world. God went about it immediately after the fall of man . . . and so will proceed to the end of the world; and then will come when the top stone shall be brought forth, and all will appear complete and consummate.

Satan, in instigating "the ruins of the fall," endeavors "to frustrate [God's] design . . . to destroy his workmanship." But Satan's efforts are doomed, for God's "glorious building" is solidly founded on "the first stone" of Christ's covenant of redemption. Christ is "the chief corner stone" of "this great building of redemption," and, Edwards explains, "if we are Christians, we belong to that building of God." In order to read history properly, therefore, we must first discover its architectural blueprint. Once we perceive this underlying design, then we shall realize how, in the structural scheme of providence, all historical events are "united, just as the several parts of one building: There are many stones, many pieces of timber, but all are so joined, and fitly framed together, that they make but one building: They have all but one foundation, and are united at last in one top stone." History, for Edwards, manifests an underlying structural stability in every way as cohesive as the inner self of the individual saint and the collective self of Puritan tradition. Nothing appears accidental or chaotic when deluding subjectivity is put aside for vision arising from one's alignment with the objective reality of God.

References to streams and oceans also frequently occur in the

History. Though conventional Puritan images, they are put to good use by Edwards. At one point in the work he reviews what he has previously written: "We began at the head of the stream of divine providence, and have followed and traced it through its various windings and turnings, till we are come to the end . . . where it issues. As it began in God, so it ends in God. God is the infinite ocean into which it empties itself." In another passage Edwards develops the image still further:

> God's providence may not unfitly be compared to a large and long river, having innumerable branches, beginning in different regions, and at a great distance one from another, and all conspiring to one common issue. After their very diverse and [apparent] contrary courses . . . they all gather more and more together, the nearer they come to their common end, and all at length discharge themselves at one mouth into the same ocean. The different streams of this river are apt to appear like mere jumble and confusion to us, because of the limitedness of our sight, whereby we cannot see from one branch to another, and cannot see the whole at once. . . . A man who sees but one or two streams at a time, cannot tell what their course tends to. Their course seems very crooked, and different streams seem to run for a while different and contrary ways: And if we view things at a distance there seem to be innumerable obstacles and impediments in the way to hinder their ever uniting and coming to the ocean, as rocks and mountains and the like; but yet if we trace them, they all unite at last, and all come to the same issue, disgorging themselves in one into the same great ocean.

It is, then, in terms of the grand design that historical events must be interpreted, otherwise they "will all look like confusion, like a number of jumbled events coming to pass without any order or method, like the tossing of the waves of the sea." These traditional images prove structurally useful to Edwards, as do the architectural analogies, because they too convey an impression of the radical order, unity, and pattern at the core of history. So closely joined are they in Edwards' mind, in fact, that he readily mixes metaphors, as in the following passage on the end of time: "now the whole work of redemption is finished. . . . Now the top stone of the building is laid. In the progress of the discourse on this subject, we have followed the church of God in all the great changes, all her tossings to and fro that she has been subject to, in all the storms and tempests through the many ages of the world, till at length we have seen an end to all these storms. We have seen her enter the harbor, and landed in the highest heavens, in complete and eternal glory." God's edifice, like Noah's ark, is brought home safely over the perilous waves of the world.

The function of these images as organizational motifs is not unique in Puritan writings. Their subtle dimension in the *History* surfaces when we realize that usually they are associated with the soul. In other words, Edwards presents the construction of God's building of redemption in terms exactly identical to those he and countless other divines before him used to describe the effects of grace in the soul. Traditionally the soul is spoken of as the temple of the Holy Spirit, and frequently it is depicted as a pilgrim tossed about on the seas of experience. By using these motifs Edwards intended, in short, to portray, through identical imagery, a correspondence between Christ's covenant of redemption with regard to history (including the church, which exists in and fulfills time) and His covenant of grace with regard to the individual elect soul. He explicitly declares his intention when he remarks: "I would observe, that the increase of gospel light, and the carrying on the work of redemption, as it respects the elect church in general, from the first erecting of the church to the end of the world, is very much after the same manner as the carrying on of the same work and the same light in a particular soul, from the time of its conversion, till it is perfected and crowned in glory." History, particularly as reflected in the progress of the church, possesses a collective self—for Edwards it was most evident in Puritan tradition —akin to the inner self of the saint; it comprises a coherent allegory of the soul's experience of grace.

Thus, even in the *History* Edwards pursues answers to the questions about conversion he raised in his college diary. Reinforcing the view set forth in *A Faithful Narrative*, he explains that the soul receives grace immediately but that its regenerative transformation requires progressive stages of development. The drama of conversion is like the unfolding of history. Both are "accomplished in various steps" and "by degrees." In both, the ultimate pattern or scheme tends to remain obscure to man, so murky that he may subjectively see it as manifesting apparent "contrary courses." Yet in fact, as Edwards notes elsewhere, "God is continually causing revolutions. Providence makes a continual progress, and continually is bringing forth things new in the state of the world, and very different from what ever were before. He removes one that He may establish another. And perfection will not be obtained till the last revolution, when God's design will be fully reached."[11] In another place Edwards speaks of the turmoil of historical events as God's new creation, a gradual re-creation, which image equally applies to the renovation of the soul through grace:

> As after nature has long been shut up in a cold dead state, in time of winter, when the sun returns in the spring, there is, together with the increase of the light and heat of the sun, very dirty and tempestuous weather, before all is settled calm and serene, and all nature rejoices in its bloom and beauty. It is in the new creation as it was in the old: the Spirit of God first moved upon the face of the waters, which was an occasion of great uproar and tumult, and things were gradually brought to a settled state.[12]

Bereft of any knowledge of this "design, it would all appear to [men] confusion," Edwards explains in the *History*: "the work in a particular soul has its ups and downs; sometimes the light shines brighter, and sometimes it is a dark time; sometimes grace seems to prevail, at other times it seems to languish for a great while together. . . . But in general, grace is growing: From its first infusion, till it is perfected in glory, the kingdom of Christ is building up in the soul."

The equation of the progress of time and the experience of the gracious soul illustrates Edwards' proneness to look within for the touchstone of reality. For him history may be real, but ultimately its meaning (like that of nature) derives from its correspondence to and revelation of the spiritual growth of the gracious soul. The saint's soul, like history, possesses meaning or identity because Christ informs its center or foundation. As the phrase "building up in the soul" implies, Edwards ultimately grounds the architectonics of the history of redemption within the terrain of the regenerate

[11] *The Philosophy of Jonathan Edwards*, p. 135. This view of history lies at the heart of Edwards' notion that the millennium is an imminent event to occur within ordinary history; see C. C. Goen, "Jonathan Edwards: A New Departure in Eschatology," *Church History* 28 (March 1959): 25–40.

[12] *Some Thoughts*, in Edwards, *The Great Awakening*, p. 318.

self. Thus, in explaining why God constructs Christ's building of redemption so gradually, he actually also probes the mystery of his own conversion experience:

> In this way the glory of God's wisdom . . . is more visible to the observation of creatures. If it had been done at once, in an instant, or in a very short time, there would not have been such opportunities for creatures to perceive and observe the particular steps of divine wisdom, as when the work is gradually accomplished, and one effect of his wisdom is held forth to observation after another. It is wisely determined of God, to accomplish his great design by a wonderful and long series of events, that the glory of his wisdom may be displayed in the whole series, and that the glory of his perfections may be seen, appearing, as it were, by parts, and in particular successive manifestations. For if all that glory which appears in all these events had been manifested at once, it would have been too much for us . . .; it would have dazzled our eyes, and overpowered our sight.

Whatever apparent meanderings the saint's life or his emotions may take, the fact remains that the rivulets of his inner being steadily flow, along with everything else in nature and history, toward the final ocean of God.

Because he discerns this correspondence, it is not surprising that Edwards applies to history his favorite image for the saint's soul. As we saw in *God Glorified*, the inner self of the elect becomes moonlike in its reflection of the divine light (which Edwards carefully defined in *A Divine and Supernatural Light*). Likewise in history, as an allegory of the blessed soul, "the light that the church enjoyed from the fall of man, till Christ came, was like the light which we enjoy in the night; not the light of the sun directly, but as reflected from the moon and stars; which light did foreshow Christ, the Sun of righteousness." In his notes on the Bible, he explains that Christ is "the Sun from whom the Church borrows her light. The gospel light granted to the Old Testament church in its different successive ages, was very much like the light of the moon in the several parts of the revolution it performs, which ends in its conjunction with the sun."[13] Even full conjunction, however, proves inadequate in terms of the total overview, as Edwards sug-

[13] *Works* (Dwight), 9:559.

gests in the *History*: "The proper time of the success or effect of Christ's purchase of redemption is after the purchase has been made, as the proper time for the world to enjoy the light of the sun is the day time, after the sun is risen, though we may have some small matter of it reflected from the moon and planets before."

Thus, just as the elect soul does not become totally illuminated until it reaches heaven, so too history is not suddenly and maximally made lucid by Christ's Incarnation. History, like the elect soul, must advance by degrees, for "the success of Christ's redemption while he himself was on earth, was very small in comparison of what it was after the conclusion of his humiliation." Christ's Incarnation, in short, is an act affecting history directly in a way similar to the immediate communication of special grace to the soul, but, with regard to both the inner self of the saint and the collective self of history, the actualization of this influence is progressive. As the soul grows in grace and as history approaches eternity, both by means of a posteriori phases, the more luminous they become.

This was Edwards' "new method." Had he lived to develop this early collection of sermons, had he had an opportunity especially to perfect many of the images that clearly convey much of his argument, he no doubt would have produced the major treatise he envisioned. By discerning in all of history an allegory of the spiritual progress of the saint's self, he sounded a prophetic note. The Old Testament prophets, he believed, "were the stars that reflected the light of the sun." He too, as Christ's ambassador, sought to shed light on the darkness he thought overshadowed New England and the world in 1739: "It is now a very dark time with respect to the interests of religion, . . . wherein there is but a little faith, and a great prevailing of infidelity on the earth." He was certain that "God in his providence now seems to be acting over again the same part which he did a little time before Christ came." As a latter-day prophet Edwards announced the second coming of Christ. He prophesied that the progress of history and the regeneration of the soul are "swiftly, yet gradually" coming to an end. He confessed that "whether the times shall be any darker still, or how much darker, before the beginning of this glorious work of

God, we cannot tell." Yet his message was clear and doubtless proved a significant element in the preparation of Northampton for another revival in the 1740's.

Edwards' prophetic duty was to help communicate Christ's redemption, both in the souls of his parishioners and thereby in the church and in history. "This is a work which will be accomplished," he told his audience, "by the preaching of the gospel, and the use of the ordinary means of grace, and so shall be gradually brought to pass." Hence Edwards' prophetic persona in the *History* is most appropriate. By this means he personally merged, as it were, his private self and the collective self of history in a single voice. As a spiritual father of New England, he derived his authority not only from Scripture but also from the twin luminaries of an inspired inner self and history, the latter an allegory of the former; as a prophetic agent of divine Will he joined the two together. In a very real sense Edwards had come to think of himself as a luminary, like the prophets of old, shedding light on God's grand architectural design.

III. *Like Such a Little Flower*

Both *A Faithful Narrative* and the *History*, as we have observed, not only pertained to the revival but also to a significant extent aided Edwards in resolving the dilemma posed by his own religious experience. Sometime during 1739 or thereabouts—the manuscript has been lost and the date cannot be satisfactorily determined—he wrote some reflections on his own spiritual progress. This document, entitled "Personal Narrative," must have been somewhat derived from his diary and possibly from journals he may have kept over the years. In spite of these likely sources and the implied act of retrospection, however, we should not expect the narrative to present a straightforward account of Edwards' experience. The "Personal Narrative" is a mature work in the sense that it was nurtured by the lessons he had learned from the revival. Like many of his other writings, it functions on two levels. Primarily it presents a somewhat formulary spiritual autobiography; less immediately evident are its conscious artistic qualities. In other words, the techniques of this document suggest that it may not have been intended to serve merely as a private record but, like the best of such accounts in Puritan New England, may have been written with an audience in mind.

In reading the "Personal Narrative" it is important to recall that by 1739 Edwards understood the drama of conversion to be progressive, even though the actual reception of grace is immediate. He now saw that the "particular steps," more likely a posteriori rather than actually preparatory, were not necessarily readily demonstrable. More often than not, he concluded, they tended to remain obscure to the very individual experiencing them. Nevertheless, though superficially stunted, such degrees of spiritual growth, especially with regard to the gradual *effects* of grace, do indeed occur. They comprise a pervasive process, a grand design within the soul of the saint. This larger pattern lies at the heart of the "Personal Narrative." Its emergence in this work, however, is as subtle as it is in the saint's actual experience. Thus Edwards avoids a neat linear sequence of events and uses a seemingly amorphous, even fragmentary narrative method in the essay. The opening sentence, for instance, is cumulative, summarizing the entire work and suggesting composite, barely discernible levels in the account to be set forth: "I had a variety of concerns and exercises about my soul from my childhood; but had two more remarkable seasons of awakening, before I met with that change by which I was brought to those new dispositions, and that new sense of things, that I have since had."[14] This sentence implies that these phases are more merged than unique, more like the indistinguishable waves of the sealike "process of time" in which the narrator finds himself.

For the most part the narrator remains baffled by these phases. As he in time increases in spiritual awareness, however, he can better fathom them and derive some inkling of their meaning. Even the saint remains for the most part trapped in the ignorance of his subjectivity, which explains why the narrator of the "Personal Narrative" remarks, concerning one facet of his early awakening, that he "never could give an account, how, or by what means, [he] was thus convinced [of the doctrine of God's sover-

[14] My source for the "Personal Narrative" is Samuel Hopkins' *Life and Character of Edwards*, pp. 24–39.

eignty]; not in the least imagining, in the time of it, nor a long time after, that there was any extraordinary influence of God's Spirit in it." In retrospect, as his self becomes more and more aligned with the objectivity of divine reality, the saint begins to discern in what respect such events play a part in God's progressive influence upon the soul. With time and relentless heart-searching, he may in fact discover, albeit without presumptuous certitude, something of a blessed design or plan in the very occurrences which had hitherto been utterly mysterious and confounding to him.

Traditionally Puritans believed that what one recorded of his spiritual motions in a diary should, upon reexamination over the years, reveal some underlying design. According to Puritan psychology, words, especially those of prayerful meditation, derive from the will or heart and inevitably reflect the moral condition of that faculty. The true meaning of these words does not necessarily correspond to the glitter of their surfaces but tends to lie buried in their deeper strata, in levels beyond the writer's control and comprehension. Only after years of heart-searching and the progressive effects of grace can the saint begin to espy this underlying design. Language, then, serves as a divine instrument instructing man about himself and about God's ways with him. Edwards, however, carefully alerts us to its limitations as well. Ultimately language communicates only reflections of the spiritual influences upon the soul. In the "Personal Narrative," consequently, he frequently speaks of the limits of language: "I know not how to express"; "what I felt within, I could not express"; "my wickedness, as I am in myself, has long appear'd to me perfectly ineffable." Language cannot finally cope with God's sovereign and mysterious providence, even though it is divinely ordained to provide clues to the spiritual condition of one's will.

The faculty of will, the principle locus of the self, is of central interest in the "Personal Narrative." The "secret corruption and deceit" that lay within the narrator's heart, that continually seemed to abort his spiritual rebirth, was "too great a dependence on [his] own strength." This manifestation of pride, the chief sin of the perverse heart, doubtless had its root in his childhood, when he took "much self-righteous pleasure" in religious duties and found his mind "full of objections against the doctrine of God's sovereignty." In retrospect, however, the narrator sees that these early vacillating spiritual experiences manifested part of the divine scheme for him. Their sealike rhythm, with its ebb and flow, was intended steadily to wear away and level his arrogant sense of self-hood. As a result, he eventually came to desire sincerely "to lie low before God, and in the dust; that I might be nothing, and that God might be all; that I might become as a little child"; "I very often think with sweetness and longings and pantings of soul, of being a little child, taking hold of Christ, to be led by Him through the wilderness of this world." As a child of God, the saint feels a help-less dependence on divine parental authority; his heart does not yet possess any real sense of self but actually engages in the process of developing an identity with Christ as its informing center.

The narrator of the "Personal Narrative" thus realizes that it is his perverse, self-righteous will which requires rectification. Owing to the progressive work of special grace, he eventually comes to feel "an ardency of soul to be, what I know not otherwise how to express, than to be emptied and annihilated; to lie in the dust, and to be full of Christ alone"; "the thought of any comfort or joy aris-ing in me, or any consideration, or reflection on my own amiable-ness, or any of my performances or experiences, or any goodness of heart or life, is nauseous and detestable to me." In contrast to his previous "vile exaltation," he now ascertains within himself a childlike search for true identity. Real selfhood, in terms of this quest, stems from a total dependence on Christ's divine Self: "I love to think of coming to Christ, to receive salvation of Him, poor in spirit, and quite empty of self; humbly exalting Him alone; cut entirely off from my own root, and to grow into, and out of Christ."

With Christ as its center, the self becomes a more immediate and intimate source of revelation than the external world. As we have been observing, Edwards increasingly came to view the saint-ly self as a singularly important key to divine reality and, there-fore, as a measure of the world in which he lived. The "Personal Narrative" confirms this direction in his thinking. In this work we again meet the boy who was fascinated by spiders, the lad attracted to the expression of Providential design in nature: "God's excel-lency, his wisdom, his purity and love, seemed to appear in every thing; in the sun, moon and stars; the clouds, and blue sky; in the grass, flowers, trees; in the water, and all nature; which used greatly to fix my mind." Such beauty *used* to fascinate him. Now that he has grown older and delved deeper into the nature of conversion, the self has emerged as a more vital vehicle of divine communication. It is this inner field of reality that he encounters when he experiences "a calm, sweet abstraction of soul from all the concerns of this world; and a kind of vision, or fix'd ideas and imaginations, of being alone in the mountains, or some solitary wilderness, far from all mankind, sweetly conversing with Christ and wrapt and swallowed up in God." Nature has been internalized; in a sense, as in *God Glorified*, it becomes transformed into a psychic landscape reflecting the inner terrain of the self. Thus the soul is "like a field or garden of God, with all manner of pleasant flowers; that is all pleasant, delightful and undisturbed; enjoying a sweet calm, and the gently vivifying beams of the sun"; it appears "like such a little flower, as we see in the spring of the year; low and humble on the ground, opening its bosom, to receive the pleasant beams of the sun's glory." The imprint of divine excellency the narrator once perceived in nature is now disclosed by the inner landscape of the self. It is, he tells us, "an inward, sweet delight in God" which lies at the center of the saint's new identity. Thunder and lightning, viewed from the new perspective of the inner self, no longer terrify him as they once did; like historical events, they become mere types or shadows of the reality revealed in the saint's soul. Nature's indictment of man, implied in "Of Insects," nearly disappears, permitting the narrator to rejoice truly in all natural phenomena. For him the gap between God and man steadily narrows because he is closing with his Creator in his heart. The distance between God and man, albeit real in one sense, is a subjective, inward gulf; it is the sin-ridden will, "an abyss infinitely deeper than hell," which accounts for one's estrangement from his divine origin.

By the time he wrote his spiritual autobiography, as we have seen, Edwards had to a considerable extent answered many of the questions he had raised about his own conversion experience. Yet nowhere in the "Personal Narrative" does he assert that he is saved. Even near the conclusion of the essay he remarks, "I am greatly afflicted with a proud and self-righteous spirit"; wickedness is "like an infinite deluge, or infinite mountains over my head." Similarly to Puritans of the preceding generations, Edwards eschewed an easy deciphering of the meaning of the spiritual phases he had undergone. Whether he had been the recipient of saving grace is one question to be answered for certain only after death, for assurance in one's election may very well testify to the damning sin of presumption. Furthermore, as he had indicated in *A Faithful Narrative* and *A History of the Work of Redemption*, the effects of grace are progressive. The work of the Holy Spirit is not completed until the soul has concluded its pilgrim's progress in this world. The saint, therefore, is to "grow in grace," his sense of divine things is to be "gradually increased."

While on earth, the saint can barely penetrate the mystery surrounding his spiritual condition. However, he may and must strive for intimations of evidence as reflected by his moonlike soul, glimpses encouraging him to hope genuinely in his salvation. Mere hints are all he can detect within the murkiness and vicissitudes of his internal disposition. When he comments that "God's absolute sovereignty, and justice, with respect to salvation and damnation, is what my mind seems to rest assured of . . . at least it is so at times," the narrator of the "Personal Narrative" confesses to an internal fluctuation, but it is a vacillation representing a normal aspect of the overall regenerative process. In a significant way, then, the heart-searching evident in the "Personal Narrative" is indicative of a proper response to grace. Appropriately its author refuses to provide any real resolution—assuming the document is intentionally fragmentary—because this meditative exercise hopefully signifies just one more phase within the more pervasive pattern of God's grand design yet to be realized in full. The saint must continue to burrow within himself, and possibly his autobiographical writings will, in retrospect, prove to be various landmarks in his spiritual progress.

It is doubtful that Edwards intended the "Personal Narrative" solely for his own benefit. The techniques of the essay suggest that he had an audience in mind. Reminiscent of "The Excellency of Christ" is his deliberate frustration of the reader's expectations. The spiritual autobiography commences with a brief account of his childhood awakenings, then abruptly announces that these "convictions and affections wore off." The story continues, explaining how, as a result of a serious illness, he "was brought wholly to break off all former wicked ways." But soon this change also passes away. This pattern is repeated a third time at greater length. The reader now learns of his encounter with "a new sort of affection," "a kind of vision," a mystical dimension in which God's excellency "seemed to appear in every thing." The narrator carefully and steadily increases the intensity of this episode, eventually implying that the Holy Spirit dwelt in his heart: "Prayer seem'd to be natural to me; as the breath, by which the inward burnings of my heart had vent." These new affections "were of a more inward, pure, soul-animating and refreshing nature." In spite of the crescendo of this latter narrative sequence and its intimated assurance, the expectations of the reader are suddenly frustrated in the next paragraph. The outcome of this jolt, this fracturing of confidence, is an inwardly felt sense on the part of the reader of what is meant when the narrator says he had placed "too great a dependence on my own strength." By permitting his expectations to depend too easily on the superficial evidence presented in the account, the narrator and the reader alike reveal a species of pride. Edwards intends to make the reader aware, at an emotional level, of how the operation of pride in the heart often eludes him, how it can cause him to repudiate unconsciously the impenetrability of and his utter dependence upon the absolute sovereignty of God's mysterious Will. Thus Edwards closes the episode by eradicating the narrator's sense of achievement, with which the reader has been identifying: "My experience had not then taught me, as it has done since, my extreme feebleness and impotence, every manner of way; and the bottomless depths of secret corruption and deceit, that there was in my heart."

In no sense, it should be noted, does Edwards discredit these experiences. He recognizes that they are phases or stages of spiritual growth in the saint. Yet he adamantly refuses to permit us to derive any fixed formula for determining that spiritual state. Deprived of such a datum, the reader is forced to experience the nature of his own insecurity. The narrator of the "Personal Narrative," unlike the prophetic persona of the *History*, is unable to

decipher God's method. The reader too, as a result of the techniques employed in the essay, shares in the narrator's plight, in his
feeling of ignorance and helplessness before God's mysterious
ways.

This effect is intensified by still another device, the obfusca-
tion of the reader's sense of past and present time. Although four
seasons of spiritual growth are delineated, the untransitioned in-
trusions of a narrator, whose controlling vision in the immediate
present encompasses any mere account of past events, contribute to
an overall fusion of these four periods. Consequently, the pattern
implied by the seasons of spiritual advancement is at best dimly
perceived. Actually the sequential development the reader has
been led to expect from the opening sentence is subverted by a near
simultaneity of time throughout the essay. Norman Grabo has
come closest to describing it: "what is missing in the *Personal Narrative* is a conventional use of time and linear dimension"; "the
process of life, the growth of spirit, is vital and dynamic; and describing it forced Edwards into a correspondingly organic form."[15]
Past, present, and future are, in a sense, merged together, for, with
regard to one's spiritual progress, time cannot be any more meaningfully factored into sequences than conversion can be delineated
in terms of specific stages. This explains why the voice of the narrator in the immediate present remains constant.[16] His presentation of time is not in accord with our customary awareness of its
sequences as measured by the world in which we live. On the contrary, he presents time as the saint comes to feel it in his heart. The
saint, beginning to transcend the subjective shackles of viewing
time as the sum total of unique stages, learns from the *timefull* terrain of the inner self that, seen from the objective reality that is
God, all points in time are merged, even identical. Thus a curious
tension emerges in the "Personal Narrative" between the voice of
the more knowledgeable speaker in the immediate present and that
of the apparently unsuspecting narrator of the past. It is precisely

[15] "Jonathan Edwards' *Personal Narrative*: Dynamic Stasis," *Literatur in
Wissenschaft und Unterricht* 2 (1969): 141–148.

[16] Daniel B. Shea, Jr., makes several insightful comments about the narrator in the "Personal Narrative" in *Spiritual Autobiography in Early America*,
pp. 187–208.

this tension, reinforced by an inward, retrospective groping which even the final speaker fails to resolve, that contributes to Edwards' aim to evoke a sense of insecurity in the reader.

The "Personal Narrative" ends abruptly, giving it the appearance of a fragment. Whether or not Edwards intended this, it is a most appropriate conclusion. It leaves the reader dangling, providing still one more frustration of his expectations and implying that there is no temporal conclusion to the regenerative process. The reader concludes the narrative, anticipating some explicit revelation of meaning, only to be left with the feeling that more is to follow. Each saint must complete his own pilgrimage on earth, in time, before the meaning of his life is fully disclosed. Total assurance of his salvation is not possible because it would yield a static condition antithetical to the progressive workings of grace. For Edwards the effects of grace, indications of its presence, develop in time.

The anticlimactic close of the "Personal Narrative" thus captures the sense of the entire document in a way no words could. It sums up the frustration of our expectations throughout the essay, the tension created by the presence of a simultaneously unsuspecting yet knowing narrator, and the confusion arising from the subversion of our normal perception of time as linear sequence. Insofar as this document possesses these aesthetic qualities, we can think of it as a conscious artistic creation informed by a principle of decorum evident elsewhere in Edwards' writings. Edwards succeeds in making the reader feel, at an intuitive even more than at a rational level, how ignorant and insecure man truly is before the mystery of the divine Will.

[4]

Affections and the Self: Writings during the Great Awakening

In the 1740's New England underwent another religious revival, one far more pervasive in its influence than any previous to it. This event, generally referred to as the Great Awakening, was not limited to a small region. To some extent this revival owed its success to the fact that by 1740 much of New England's religious fervor had declined and was ripe for renewal. Equally significant was the emergence of itinerant preachers as catalytic agents, many of whom had not been ordained in accord with older Puritan customs. These men usually preached extemporaneously with much emotion. Their sermons, generally accented by a dramatic raising and lowering of the minister's voice and frequently accompanied by expressive physical gestures, tended to emphasize the terrors of hell awaiting the impenitent sinner. They were, in content and manner of delivery, aimed at the emotions rather than at the intellect of the hearer.

Of all of these men, George Whitefield was doubtless the most influential. An Englishman sympathetic to the Methodist movement, he visited the American colonies, where he succeeded in awakening many souls. Arriving in Northampton on October 17, 1740, he stayed with Edwards for three days and preached several sermons before the congregation. Edwards had been deeply disappointed that his parishioners had fallen into a "low state" since the earlier revival in the town. But as a result of Edwards' endeavor to keep a spark of this former piety aglow, Whitefield encountered no obstacles to his success in rekindling the spiritual embers of the Northampton laity.

In the wake of Whitefield's visit, Edwards found himself a participant in the Great Awakening, though it is important to bear in mind that he always remained a tradition-oriented moderate who could readily descry faults in the extreme positions of both the defenders and the detractors of the revival (that is, of the New and the Old Lights). In order to cultivate the effect of Whitefield's preaching, he delivered a number of imprecatory sermons stressing the terrors of the damned in hell. A good example of these sermons is "The Future Punishment of the Wicked Unavoidable and Intolerable," which he delivered six months after Whitefield's departure.

I. *In Chains of Darkness*

"The Future Punishment of the Wicked" clearly asserts the righteousness of God in damning sinners to eternal torment. Less immediately apparent is its emphasis on two types of liberty which the self can know. Perhaps the easiest approach to this facet of the sermon is to recall John Winthrop's definition of natural and federal liberties. Natural liberty, according to Winthrop, refers to man's freedom "to do what he lists," a license by means of which "men grow more evil."[1] Civil or federal liberty, on the other hand, represents "the proper end and object of authority . . . it is a liberty to that only which is good, just, honest" and it is maintained "in a way of subjection to authority." This traditional understanding of liberty underlies Edwards' portrait of the self in "The Future Punishment of the Wicked."

The beginning of the sermon stresses the relation between natural liberty and sinners' foolish assertions of selfhood. Because the wicked will not bear authority of any sort, "they baffle all the means used with them by those that are appointed to teach and to rule over them. They will not yield to parents, or to the counsels,

[1] Winthrop's speech before the General Court (July 3, 1645), from which the following quotations are taken, appears in Perry Miller and Thomas H. Johnson, eds., *The Puritans*, 1:205–207.

warnings, or reproofs of ministers."[2] By renouncing the legitimate authority of their natural and spiritual parents, these obdurate individuals actually repudiate or "make nothing of God's authority," for parental government is an earthly surrogate for divine jurisdiction. Manifesting a perverse sense of will, they blind themselves to the fact that everything, most of all one's self, is totally dependent on God's sovereign Will. They thus become rebels who, like Satan, pridefully plot insurrection: "they despise God in their hearts, and have the weapons of war about them, though they are secret enemies, and carry their swords under their skirts"; "they always continue to oppose and resist God as long as they live in the world; they never lay down the weapons of their rebellion."[3]

Edwards extends this military metaphor to incorporate an economic one likewise depicting the essentially criminal nature of the sinner. The wicked "are continually plunging themselves deeper and deeper in debt, and at the same time imagine they shall escape the payment of the debt, and design entirely to rob God of his due." Pride and presumption go hand-in-hand in the perverse self. Since the sinner is a rebel and a thief, he dwells outside the well-governed city of God. This fact will be particulary evident at the Last Judgment, when the damned will, like the animals with whom they share natural liberty, struggle "to hide themselves in some cave or den of the mountains, or in any secret hole of the earth."

In accord with the absolute order requisite to divine justice, such foolish freedom will be followed by coerced submission: "If they will not be willing subjects to the golden sceptre, and will not yield to the attractives of his love, they shall be subject to the force of the iron rod, whether they will or no." At the end of the world, Edwards explains in terms of his military metaphor, God "will gird himself with might," and "His sword is not the sword of man." Then each debt of every thieving rebel will be taken into

[2] This sermon is printed in *Works* (Austin), 7:375–395.

[3] This and several other images are mentioned in another context in James C. Cowan, "Jonathan Edwards' Sermon Style: 'The Future Punishment of the Wicked Unavoidable and Intolerable,'" *South Central Bulletin* 29 (Winter 1969): 119–122. Clyde A. Holbrook discusses Edwards' idea of virtue as a vision of harmony in contrast to subjective anarchy in "Edwards and the Ethical Question," *Harvard Theological Review* 60 (April 1967): 163–175.

account and collected: "All their sins are written in his book; not one of them is forgotten, and every one must be paid"; "their sins must be fully balanced, and recompensed, and satisfaction obtained." The honor of God, Edwards warns, will "in due time be vindicated" and then the wicked will find themselves "subdued and convicted." The ultimate payment for living in the false liberty of rebellion is an eternal loss of freedom: "Nor will they ever be able to make their escape. They will find no means to break prison and flee. In hell they will be reserved in chains of darkness for ever and ever." So confined, the prisoners of hell are deprived of true selfhood—the very thing they mistakenly thought they possessed when engaged in sin. Defenseless, helpless, selfless, they must endure the naked exposure of their hearts, the "inmost closet" of which is eternally "open" to God. The ultimate irony of their situation arises from the fact that whereas they once could have striven to renounce false selfhood voluntarily, now that repudiation is forced upon them through the inevitable humiliation of the prideful will, a humiliation which comes too late for them to benefit from it.

Edwards develops this theme further by referring throughout the work to the image of hands which he derives from Ezek. 12:14. As we noted elsewhere, Puritans believed that one's thoughts, words, and deeds comprise the gamut of the heart's expression. It follows that whatever is performed by one's hands—a conventional synecdoche for one's deeds—must in some way testify to the spiritual disposition of the will motivating them. It is quite consistent, therefore, that the rebels portrayed in "The Future Punishment of the Wicked" reveal pride in the belief that "their hands be strong to deliver them" from divine wrath. But swords in the hands of the wicked amount to nothing in the end because their self-reliant hearts are not aligned to the divine Self, whence true identity and strength arise. The unregenerate eventually discover God to be more than equal to the challenge of their insurrection, learning that actually they are inescapably "in the hands of the great God." At the Last Judgment battle will not even commence, as rebel "hands . . . drop down at once." With the skirmish preempted, the insurgents realize there is "no strength in their hands to do any thing to appease God." Finally imprisoned in hell, where "the torment will be immensely beyond their strength," they painfully discover "what a poor hand" they make "at fighting with the flames." In hell the heart of stone and its hardened resolves, previously the support of the rebel, "will become like wax before the furnace."

In contrast to the unregenerate are the elect, who renounce natural liberty for federal liberty during their earthly life. They embrace divine authority joyfully, resigning themselves to it. With the aid of special grace they voluntarily repudiate a false sense of selfhood. Once their hearts are properly disposed, the saints steadily progress toward the attainment of genuine self-identity rooted in Christ. In every way the elect become "willing subjects" yielding their wills to "the attractives of [divine] love."

As we have seen, specifically in *God Glorified* and the "Personal Narrative," the child is Edwards' chief image for this reformed state of the self. The saint must turn to God as a child looks to his parents for instruction and guidance in forming a proper self-identity. Throughout his writings he likewise refers to the sinner as "a child of the devil." The unregenerate self is modelled after "the father of all sin," the "grand rebel,"[4] for, as Edwards explains in an undated sermon on Acts 16:29–30, the wicked "subject themselves to him, hearken to his counsels, as children hearken to the counsels of a father. They learn of him to imitate him, and do as he does, as children learn to imitate their parents." Without grace the heart "of a natural man is the habitation of the devil. The devil is not only their father, and rules over them, but he dwells in them." Deprived of the indwelling Holy Spirit the soul does not serve as the temple of God but as "the synagogue of Satan," which in typological terms means that it exists in a pre-Christian state.[5]

With the subjugation of the rebellious self at the Last Judgment, when it is too late to benefit them, the children of Satan realize their proper parentage. Then, Edwards makes clear in "The Future Punishment of the Wicked," they will see "how little are they in the hands of the great God! they are less than weak infants." Even the strongest of them will possess "no more courage

4 *Works* (Austin), 7:229, 232.
5 Quotations from this sermon are from *Works* (Dwight), 8:14, 15.

than the feeblest infant." Because it comes too late, this discovery
of weakness metamorphoses into a fatal indictment for the sinner,
in contrast to the redeemed, for whom it is merely a confirmation
and an occasion for joy. A coerced childlike relationship, a forced
humiliation of the rebellious heart, serves as an eternal ironic
reminder to the damned of the chance they once had to accept
this relationship to God voluntarily. The irony is compounded by
their sentence to everlasting imprisonment, in which condition the
soul is forever denied selfhood, even in its perverse manifestations,
for not even prideful anger can withstand the flames of hell. There
the condemned will truly learn what it means to yield the heart,
and because the lesson will not resolve their quest for selfhood, it
only increases their misery. The fulfillment of divine intent requires that every heart be subdued and that every person eventually recognize his subordinate, childlike relation to God. The
unregenerate learn everything too late, and the completion of the
grand design of Providence only presses their indictment further.

In "The Future Punishment of the Wicked," the minister's
voice is referred to as "the roaring of heaven's cannon," implying
its relation to the divine army that is to rout the insurgents. Yet
Edwards carefully shuns any hint of pride on his part. A few lines
after the preceding phrase he suggests that it is commonly God's
method "to let men try their utmost strength; particularly to let
ministers try, that thus he may show ministers their own weakness
and impotency; and when they have done what they can, and all
fails, then God takes the matter into his own hands." Edwards
was applying the message of the sermon to himself as much as to
his parishioners. In the midst of the new awakening he wanted to
remain humble, taking no credit for himself and striving to avoid
the delusions which had accompanied the revival of the 1730's.
Without Christ as its informing center, the minister's will remains
powerless and its handiwork (thoughts, words, deeds) comes to
nothing. Edwards was still very much concerned about the spiritual disposition of his own self.

II. *Shadows and Dreams*

Of all of Edwards' sermons the one he delivered on July 8,
1741, at Enfield, Connecticut, has received most critical attention.
Derived from a version preached a month earlier in Northampton,

Sinners in the Hands of an Angry God is an imprecatory discourse and, like "The Future Punishment of the Wicked," less concerned with analyzing the nature of conversion than with preparing souls for the work of the Holy Spirit. The people of Enfield had evidently not yet been inflamed by the new revivalism, and through this sermon Edwards hoped to transform their spiritual lassitude. Unlike Whitefield, Edwards delivered his sermons in a sober and moderate tone of voice, avoiding demonstrative physical gestures. Yet the Enfield sermon proved an overwhelming success because of an inner drama conveyed through its imagery and style.[6] *Sinners* was so dramatically effective, in fact, that at one point—so we are told by such witnesses as the Reverend Eleazar Wheelock and Stephen Williams—the sighing and weeping of the congregation in attendance made it necessary for Edwards to interrupt the sermon and request silence so that he might continue.

The theme of the discourse asserts that God's pleasure alone prevents the wicked from falling into hell at any particular moment. It is just a matter of time before divine justice seeks retribution. A person never knows when that moment will arrive, although it is most likely to occur when he least expects it. The fundamental premise of the sermon is the same as that of nearly all of Edwards' writings: God's absolute sovereignty, "arbitrary will," and "unsearchable ways," resulting in man's utter dependence on Him.[7]

Many of the underlying structural devices in this work are identical to the images used in "The Future Punishment of the Wicked." Edwards once again depicts (1) how the efforts of human hands prove useless in comparison to the invincible action of divine Providence, (2) how the rebel sinner plotting insurrection encounters only defeat and punishment, and (3) how the wicked become the children of Satan rather than the adopted heirs of Christ. These motifs, as we have noted, underscore Edwards' presentation of the wicked's erroneous and fatal sense of selfhood.

For the purpose of portraying this false notion of self, Edwards

6 Edwin H. Cady offers several useful observations on the imagery of this sermon in "The Artistry of Jonathan Edwards," *New England Quarterly* 22 (March 1949): 61–72.

7 This sermon appears in *Works* (Austin), 7:486–502. The last five paragraphs are missing from this edition, however, and for them I relied on Dwight's version (*Works*, 5:175–176).

develops the image of the sleeping man which he derived from the Pauline epistles. The image operates in this sermon at both a literal and a figurative level. The literal plane is evident when Edwards pointedly observes that it is entirely owing to God's Will "that you did not go to hell the last night; that you was suffered to awake again in this world." Carefully managing this image, he transforms it into a metaphor which yokes man's physical and spiritual being. At this figurative level sleep characterizes the day-to-day activities in which every man is engaged, especially when these activities delusively support the prideful dream that he amounts to something as a personal entity. Feelings of independence and of security, Edwards warns, represent "vain dreams" or "nothing but a shadow"—that is, they are equivalent to sleep. As Edwards saw it, the helplessness and unawareness accompanying our actual sleep represent precisely the features of the life we lead when we are allegedly awake. It is, then, at the level of metaphor —albeit, as seen from God's point of view, the ultimate literal level —that Edwards appeals to his listeners to "awake thoroughly out of sleep."

Another series of images relating to sight reinforces the sleep motif. Just as one does not see when he is literally asleep, so likewise he remains blind to God's "unsearchable ways" while he is seemingly awake—that is, at the figurative level, while he sleepwalks through his daily chores and pleasures. Absorbed in the sleep of their subjective daily life, "unconverted men walk over the pit of hell on a rotten covering, and there are innumerable places in this covering so weak that they will not bear their weight, and these places are not seen." So oblivious are they to the objective reality of God that the sightless condition of their sleepwalking persists even at the most illuminated period of the day, with the consequence that "the arrows of death fly unseen at noonday." "Unexpected" and undetected while men sleep, death and eternal damnation operate like "a thief" (cf. 1 Thes. 5:4).

God is, of course, the eternal eye. His fiery vision peers into every corner of the world and of the heart. He possesses "purer eyes" than can "bear to have you in his sight." At the Last Judgment the unregenerate will be confronted and then indicted by God's vision. They will also have *their* eyes opened. However, as we saw in "The Future Punishment of the Wicked," such coerced rectification ironically serves only to increase their misery. Addressing those of his audience who have not yet experienced spiritual insight, Edwards warns that in hell the condemned will be painfully wide awake: "you shall see a long forever, a boundless duration before you, which will swallow up your thoughts, and amaze your soul; and you will absolutely despair of ever having any deliverance." Eventually everyone will discern God's scheme, but the wicked will wish they had never had their vision perfected and, starkly sensitive to the torments of hell, they will hopelessly long for the release of an eternal sleep.

Other images, the ones generally mentioned by most critics of this sermon, similarly convey an impression of human insecurity. We have already remarked a passage referring to man's precarious ambulation over the rotting cover over hell. Related to this portrait of human blindness and insufficiency is the image of a man slipping without the aid of anything that might prevent or even lessen his fall. For still another image of human helplessness, Edwards devised an analogy between men and spiders. At first he introduces this analogy obliquely, indicating how easily we may "cut or singe a slender thread that any thing hangs by." Soon the reader is led to the discovery that he is more intimately tied to this thread than he initially suspected, for now he learns that his self-righteousness has "no more influence to uphold [him] and keep [him] out of hell, than a spider's web would have to stop a falling rock." Then, almost before he realizes it, he finds himself equated with spiders, both dangling on a slender fragile thread. God, Edwards writes, "holds you over the pit of hell, much as one holds a spider, or some loathsome insect, over the fire." Whereas at first Edwards' image intimated that fate was in our hands, that we did the singeing of the arachnid, he soon frustrates this covert impression by placing us in God's hands from which we find ourselves hanging by a tenuous thread "with flames of divine wrath flashing about it, and ready every moment to singe it." Edwards' control and development of this image are genuinely artistic.

Imagery represents one means whereby Edwards gave dramatic vitality to the doctrines presented in *Sinners*. He also made effective use of the second person pronoun. It is, however, with regard to his rhetorical arrangements that he reveals another facet of his artistry similar to that manifested in "The Excellency of Christ" and *A Divine and Supernatural Light*.[8] Consider the following brief passage from the sermon: "thus it is, that natural men are held in the hand of God over the pit of hell; they have deserved the fiery pit, and are already sentenced to it." Typifying in small a technique employed throughout the discourse, this sentence is made up of three sections, each of which sequentially heightens the reader's feeling of insecurity: to be held in God's hand saps the reader of self-reliance; to be deserving of damnation redoubles this impression of helplessness; but to be already condemned expunges whatever vestige of self may yet persist. The rhetorical effect of this sentence is identical to Edwards' careful use of the spider-man analogy.

He puts this technique to excellent use as a structural device in the application section of the sermon. He arranges this section in four parts which increasingly convey the desperation of the damned. Explaining first of all "whose wrath it is," Edwards then discusses how fierce it will be. Both of these subdivisions, however, leave the reader fairly distant from the doctrine compared to Edwards' third point, which focuses on the misery to be endured by the condemned. By the time he presents the concluding item, the eternal duration of this suffering, the reader has become personally included in the expanding rhetorical web of the sermon.

One final illustration of Edwards' use of this technique in this work is worth noting: "There is the dreadful pit of the glowing flames of the wrath of God; there is hell's wide gaping mouth open; and you have nothing to stand upon, nor any thing to take hold of: There is nothing between you and hell but the air." This carefully constructed sentence ascends, as it were, in its devastating assault on the reader's sense of self. The incantatory parallelism of its sections, reinforced by dramatic images of man's diminishing security, is intended to engender an inwardly felt sensation in the audience. Edwards wanted the congregation to feel as well as to

---

[8] Willis J. Buckingham discusses Edwards' stylistic repetition and cadence in "Stylistic Artistry in the Sermons of Jonathan Edwards," *Papers in Language and Literature* 6 (Spring 1970): 136–151.

understand that the unregenerate self lacks any stabilizing context for identity. The wicked walk amid shadows, as if in a dream, where even the apparent solidity of the earth beneath their feet would dissolve upon their waking. They are out of touch with God, Who is reality.

In Edwards' view, as we have been noting, nature fails to provide man with any reality by means of which he can attain genuine self-identity. Nature may be the language of God, a revelation confirming Scripture, but since the fall man is disfranchised from the ultimate divine reality to which it bears witness. Nature, since it still retains an harmonious relation with its Creator, far from offering man a sense of security, in fact contributes to his indictment:

> Were it not that so is the sovereign pleasure of God, the earth would not bear you one moment; for you are a burden to it; the creation groans with you; the creature is made subject to the bondage of your corruption, not willingly; the sun does not willingly shine upon you to give you light to serve sin and Satan; the earth does not willingly yield her increase to satisfy your lusts; nor is it willingly a stage for your wickedness to be acted upon; the air does not willingly serve you for breath to maintain the flame of life in your vitals, while you spend your life in the service of God's enemies. God's creatures are good, and were made for men to serve God with, and do not willingly subserve to any other purpose, and groan when they are abused to purposes so directly contrary to their nature and end.

Thus, were man to look to nature in his pursuit of identity, he would perceive only his own imperfection and the consequent distance between himself and God. What alienates man from God and from the divine excellency reflected in nature is the rebellious condition of the sin-ridden heart.

For Edwards, then, the gracious heart reveals divine reality more vitally than does nature. This is why his use of nature imagery increasingly tends to define the psychic landscape rather than to refer to nature per se. Internalization of this sort occurs in *Sinners* when Edwards speaks of hell as both an exterior and an interior reality. "There are in the souls of wicked men," he argues, "those hellish principles reigning, that would presently kindle and flame out into hell fire, if it were not for God's restraints"; "the

fire pent up in their own hearts is struggling to break out." Elsewhere he similarly remarks, somewhat more cautiously:

> Natural men have, as it were, the seeds of hell within their own
> hearts. These principles of sin and corruption, which are in them,
> if they remain unmortified, will at length breed the torment of
> hell in them, and that necessarily, and of their own tendency. The
> soul that remains under the power of sin will at length take fire
> of itself. Hell will kindle in them.[9]

Since the heart of the unregenerate man is the synagogue of the
devil, it is understandable why the damned will be "tormented in
a flame that burns within them, as well as round about them."[10]
In *Sinners*, therefore, Edwards readily transforms his reference to
the literal oven of hell into a symbol (albeit equally literal in another sense) for the internal condition of the wicked: "if sin was
not restrained, it would immediately turn the soul into a fiery
oven, or a furnace of fire and brimstone." To what last threads of
security could his audience have clung as they felt the fires of hell
burning within their very breasts?

The direction of Edwards' thinking is clear. The sinner's subjective relation to hell provides the foundation for the erroneous
self-identity on which he relies. Subjectivity is all man has—this is
evident in Edwards' adaptation of Lockean notions of sensation,
particularly in his emphasis on sight imagery throughout his
writings. The context of that subjectivity, whether it is grounded
on a willful and blinding delusion of independence or on a childlike openness and submission to the divine Self, distinguishes the
damned from the elect. For Edwards it is the inner self or heart
which reveals the divine reality underlying all creation. If there is
a gap between God and man it exists not at all inherently in the
phenomenal world, in the difference between things finite and
infinite, but in the hearts of the unregenerate.

As dire as *Sinners* seems, it does not lack a glimmer of hope.
It stresses the importance of seizing the present moment and
awaking from the delusive sleep of self-righteousness. "Now you
have an extraordinary opportunity," Edwards advises his audience,
"a day wherein Christ has thrown the door of mercy wide open,

9 *Works* (Dwight), 8:22.
10 Ibid., 7:395.

and stands in calling and crying with a loud voice to poor sinners."
If they consider the revival underway in the towns in their
vicinity, he suggests, the people of Enfield have reason to hope that
they too may benefit. Yet, in typical fashion, Edwards qualifies
even this expectation. Yes, he seems to say with Pauline urgency,
there is hope but only, as it were, in terms of a single day: "What
would not those poor damned hopeless souls give for one day's
opportunity such as you now enjoy!" The "day of mercy" of which
he is speaking is literally and metaphorically a brief one. Now, this
very day of July may quite likely be the last chance for the Enfield
congregation, and this day is already rapidly passing. "God seems
now to be hastily gathering in his elect in all parts of the land," he
warns, "and probably the greater part of adult persons that ever
shall be saved, will be brought in now in a little time." As his audience listened, they no doubt reflected less upon the specific millen-
nial implications of these words than on how few were the remaining hours of sunlight for that very day. Soon they would retire
for the night, perhaps never to awaken either in the physical or
in the spiritual sense. No wonder several of those in attendance
were moved to tears.

III. *Like the Coats of an Onion*

Serious excesses multiplied in both the pulpit and the pew
during the Great Awakening. Many ministers, poorly imitating
Whitefield's techniques, tended to overdramatize their delivery of
sermons. Many of the laity too were prone to exhibit evidence of
their conversion. Such displays as fainting, crying out, and con-
vulsions were accepted by some as reputable signs of saving grace.
Furthermore, some of the laity, inflamed by religious fervor, began
to preach with an authority hitherto reserved only for properly
educated and duly ordained ministers. There had been instances
of lay preaching before the Awakening, to be sure, but they were
never very influential. Now the problem had worsened, and by the
time more conservative clergy, the Old Lights, made an effort to
correct these errors, irreparable damage had been done. Ministerial
authority was greatly impaired as a result of this emphasis on one's
private and immediate communion with the Holy Spirit.

Emphasizing one strand of traditional Puritan thought, the

Old Lights favored a more rationally restrained piety. In traditional Puritan thought, as we have noted, it was considered that reason was among Adam's chief prelapsarian attributes, that it tended hierarchically to precede the will and the affections (albeit not operating separately from them), and that it reflected the divine image within man. When Adam fell, reason was blinded. Particularly the hierarchy was destroyed, with the result that the affections, in the guise of perverted passions, now reigned over man in reason's stead. Grace, however, initiated the rectification of this condition, restoring something of the original inner hierarchy in the saint. The Old Lights, encouraged by the philosophic trend of the time, naturally concluded that the elect would lead orderly lives governed by reason; they would not be subject to violent emotional turbulence or irrational demonstrations, because these were symptoms of the dominance of the passions or of the imagination and thereby signs of internal disorder. The Old Lights were convinced, and not without cause, that such expressions of emotion could lead to spiritual and emotional anarchy. Since grace begins the restoration of the inner hierarchy, they concluded, the saints would become exemplary members of an orderly society founded on the principles of authority. The Old Lights' stress on reason, it should be noted, inevitably exaggerated the role of this faculty to the extent that they diverged from orthodox Puritan thought in several respects, especially concerning the relation between man's rationally motivated good works and conversion. Nevertheless, the premise of their thinking was indeed traditional.

Because of his role in the Northampton revival of the 1730's as well as the Great Awakening, Edwards was involved in the controversy between the Old and the New Lights. Although agreeing with the traditional grounds on which the Old Lights founded their position, he did not support their conclusions. His own spiritual experience and those of his parishioners argued against a too explicit reliance on man's rational abilities. Reason was indeed involved in the drama of conversion, but its function was certainly more difficult to define than the Old Lights suggested and in no sense did it render any man capable of assuming an active part in obtaining grace. Edwards, however, was not prepared to advocate everything condoned by the New Lights, despite his sympathy for many of their ideas. He was, in short, a tradition-oriented moderate who sought a *via media* between the extremes of the two positions.

Late in 1741 he published *The Distinguishing Marks of a Work of the Spirit of God*, followed in 1743 (not 1742, the usually assigned date) by *Some Thoughts Concerning the Present Revival of Religion in New-England* and in 1746 by *A Treatise Concerning Religious Affections*.[11] More concerned with the psychology of conversion than with theological metaphysics, these works were simultaneously public and personal documents for Edwards. Although primarily designed to help resolve the disputes between the Old and the New Lights, they are underscored by a private motivation. Just how personal these investigations were to their author is suggested by a prefatory remark made in *Religious Affections*: "The consideration of these things has long engaged me to attend this matter, with the utmost diligence and care, and exactness of search and inquiry, that I have been capable of: it is a subject on which my mind has been peculiarly intent, ever since I first entered on the study of divinity." Thus these public works bear upon Edwards' inner search for self-definition, especially as reflected in his collegiate resolutions. They reveal many of the concerns prevalent throughout his early writings, though they lack for the most part any sign of the artistic experiments which the best of these previous works manifest.

Distinguishing Marks again presents Edwards' rejection of the notion that conversion must occur in certain steps or stages. Although God's ways are progressive, as he had dramatized in the "Personal Narrative," they do not necessarily conform to human expectations or conceptions of order. There is, to be sure, design behind the operations of Providence, but the divine order is enshrouded in mysterious complexity that is certainly not reducible to simple linear terms. Man sees through a glass darkly, and if he expects "to see a work of God without difficulties and stumbling blocks, that will be like the fool's waiting at the riverside to have the water all run by."

[11] *Distinguishing Marks* and *Some Thoughts* have been reprinted in Edwards, *The Great Awakening*, ed. C. C. Goen, pp. 214–530. The edition cited for the treatise is Edwards, *Religious Affections*, ed. John E. Smith.

Underlying this point is Edwards' belief in conversion as a process that, properly considered, cannot be outlined with certitude. Not only does the experience differ from one person to another, but it remains utterly enigmatic even to the saint undergoing it. This means, finally, that the divine scheme may well include both extraordinary conversions of the sort prevalent during the revival and reasonably calm experiences such as the Old Lights defended and, hopefully, his own typified. There is no way, Edwards was sure, for anyone on earth to judge for certain what any particular spiritual occurrence signifies. However, as he dramatized in the "Personal Narrative," many of these events may in retrospect begin to form some pattern discernible to reason, thereby providing clues to the overall design. Scripture, moreover, lent its authority to the more enthusiastic responses evident during the Awakening; it indicates that at the commencement of the Holy Spirit's final influx into the world—one also should keep in mind Edwards' analogy between historical progress and spiritual regeneration—"the manner of the work will be very extraordinary, and such as never has yet been seen."

Edwards therefore saw the revival as a crucial event in the divine purpose behind history. God is methodical; yet His manner is all-inclusive, and everything serves His ends, even if it currently bewilders human perspective and comprehension. Consequently, Edwards resisted polarizing his response to the controversy. He permitted the Old Lights to maintain their notion of the calm sequential scheme of conversion while warning them that an excessive emphasis on prudence may in effect retard the Spirit's work. He agreed as well with the New Lights' view of the genuineness of extraordinary experiences while admonishing them to beware spiritual pride in new converts. He did not reject out of hand all such manifestations as visions and trances; he remained sceptical, neither dismissing nor approving. He was confirmed in the belief that such exhibitions "are no *sure* signs of their being revelations from heaven" (italics added). As a moderate who personally had witnessed the unreliability of such evidence during the aftermath of the earlier revival in Northampton, Edwards did not wish to negate entirely the role of reasonable prudence. Total abandonment to mental impressions and impulses would be analogous to ignoring "the guidance of the polar star to follow a Jack-with-a-lanthorn." In brief, the emotionalism of the revival was to be admitted, though not ignorantly without reservations; it was to be tempered by wisdom and discretion.

In *Some Thoughts* Edwards further develops ideas expressed in *Distinguishing Marks*. He again defends enthusiastic responses to grace as proper reactions in many cases. In an effort to counter the Old Light overemphasis on the methodical stages of conversion, he proclaims "that which is called a being prudent and regular, which is so much insisted on, is no other than being asleep, or cold and dead in religion." This is strong language, even though Edwards is not opposed to moderate rational restraint. He is refuting the idea that the emotions are to be entirely repressed, that they are illegitimate components in the drama of conversion. In Edwards' opinion—and he was now certainly addressing personal concerns as much as public ones—the Old Lights focus too much on the methodical regularity of the stages of conversion. In doing so they are prone to evaluate the experience a priori, that is, in terms of its means. But God's ways prove mysterious to the postlapsarian human mind cloaked in darkness. Man, as a result, catches only glimpses of the divine scheme, and such insight always derives from hindsight. This means that conversion experiences must be evaluated a posteriori or according to whatever effects they produce in the whole man. The saintly self is like the collective self of history; both should be appraised retrospectively with regard to their fruits. Thus, at the very beginning of *Some Thoughts*, Edwards argues vehemently that the revival itself should be judged in this manner: "we are to observe the effect wrought; and if, upon examination of that, it be found to be agreeable to the Word of God, we are bound without more ado to rest in it as God's work." Edwards never abandons the idea of progressive stages of growth in the soul; he merely stresses, in contrast to the Old Lights, those developments *subsequent to* the reception of saving grace as the best index to the spiritual condition of the soul, thereby in effect extricating these stages from the problematic concept of preparation.

As in *Distinguishing Marks*, he criticizes not only the Old Lights, but also the excesses of religious exuberance encouraged by many of the New Lights. It is a grave error, Edwards cautions in *Some Thoughts*, to believe that " 'tis God's manner, now in these days to guide his saints, at least some that are more eminent, by inspiration, or immediate revelation." This antinomian belief represents, in his opinion, a pernicious form of presumption; among other things it repudiates the role of ordained ministers as spiritual fathers, whose traditional importance to the Puritan mission in New England attests to God's sanction of their authority. Extraordinary experiences are frequently legitimate, but they must be scrutinized carefully. In no instance are they absolutely essential to a genuine conversion. Positioning himself between the New and the Old Lights, Edwards concludes *Some Thoughts* with a plea for the "confessing of faults on both sides."

While Edwards obviously sympathized with the New Lights because of their reassertion of certain traditional elements, whenever they diverged significantly from Puritan orthodoxy in thought or practice he tended to part company with them. A pertinent instance of disagreement occurs in *Some Thoughts*, when he defines the appropriate training and proper authorization of ministers. During the Awakening, as I just suggested, the power of the minister declined as a natural consequence of the emphasis on one's personal encounter with the Holy Spirit and the resulting equality of all the saints. The minister was becoming less and less the voice of authority in the community. In fact, if he were suspected of not having an experiential knowledge of grace or if his dogma proved unpopular, he could find himself on the defensive. Then, too, the increasing numbers of lay exhorters, unordained men acting as ministers, further undercut the older system. Such men were not without precedent in New England—Josiah Oakes of Billingsgate, for instance, was a lay exhorter who had been preaching since 1714—but during the Great Awakening they became a menace to the established clergy. Whereas many factions of the New Lights encouraged these developments, Edwards clung to the image of the duly ordained minister as the only person authorized to fill the role of spiritual father. He reasserted the traditional claim that ministers are the "ambassadors" or "officers of Christ's kingdom, that above all other men upon earth do represent his person, into whose hands Christ has committed the sacred oracles and holy ordinances, and all his appointed means of grace, to be administered by them." This was not the trend of thought among many of the New Lights, who regarded themselves as successors of Saint Paul or John the Baptist. But, for Edwards, "ministers have the charge of the house of God, which is the gate of heaven."

Such responsibility requires that the minister be trained so that he will do more good than harm in his community. Edwards' moderate viewpoint permits him to allow "that there may probably be some persons in the land, that have had no education at college, that are in themselves better qualified for the work of the ministry than some others that have taken their degrees, and are now ordained." Nevertheless, this is an uncomfortable concession for Edwards, and he instinctively defends the older view. He has no affinity for those forces aiming to "break down that fence" of tradition: "I believe the breaking over those bounds that have hitherto been set, in ordaining such persons, would in its consequences be a greater calamity, than the missing [of] such persons in the work of the ministry," because "opening a door for the admission of unlearned men to the work of the ministry, though they should be persons of extraordinary experience," will generally lead others to "impulses, vain imaginations, superstition, indiscreet zeal, and such like extremes." The implications of Edwards' choice of images are inescapable. His conservatism on this issue is reinforced by his conception of the ministry as the force of reason participating in the communal self, as the prudent restraint needed to limit the excesses of erroneous religious enthusiasm in congregations. If the minister is himself subject to such emotional enthusiasm, he will be unable to perform this protective function. This is why in two ordination sermons, *The True Excellency of a Minister of the Gospel* (August 30, 1744) and "The Church's Marriage to Her Sons, and to Her God" (September 19, 1746), Edwards reiterates his belief that ministerial piety should always be tempered with discretion. An established ministry, in his view, is a fundamental cornerstone in the architectonic of the divine scheme. As spiritual fathers, as types of Christ, Puritan ministers derive their authority from and continue to perpetuate the collective self revealed in the continuity of the traditions of their faith.

Edwards also refuted another increasingly popular notion among many New Lights and their laity, namely that a minister who has not experienced conversion is of no benefit to his parishioners. In order to lead others to salvation, the argument went, a minister must have experienced the Spirit's work. Edwards was certain that the older understanding of this problem was more accurate. Those ministers who may in fact lack saving grace, he explained, can still serve as agents of the divine Will. It is a mistaken idea to think that the state of a minister's soul hampers the operation of grace in the souls of the laity. An insecure or doubtful man in such an office, Edwards readily conceded, could do considerable damage; yet, he again reminded his readers to remember that God's ways are mysterious. Just as He may make excellent use of lay exhorters, so too He can employ unregenerate clergy. It is the minister's effect that matters, not his preceding condition—another application of Edwards' belief that the evaluation of something should be made a posteriori rather than a priori.

Edwards is certain, of course, that the best ministers are themselves members of the elect. Frequently, when speaking of the ministry, he resorts to an image he usually associates with the soul infused with grace. Ministers, he comments in *The True Excellency of a Minister of the Gospel*, "are set by Christ to be lights or luminaries in the spiritual world. . . . they are set to be that to men's souls, that the lights of heaven are to their bodies."[12] Similarly he writes elsewhere: "the moon well represents the glory of the prophets and apostles and other ministers of Christ that have been improved as such lights of his church and instruments of promoting and establishing his kingdom and glory, and so have been luminous to enlighten the world by reflecting the light of the sun that is of Christ, and conveying his beams to them."[13] Edwards applies this image to the clergy, even as he does to the souls of the elect, because they are vitally in touch with and representatives of the collective self of Puritan history. As a result of the light of divine

[12] *Works* (Austin), 8:368.
[13] *Images or Shadows of Divine Things*, p. 60.

reality which they reflect, they become, like the inner self of the saint, a source of revelation. Three years earlier, in a funeral sermon entitled *The Resort and Remedy of Those That Are Bereaved by the Death of an Eminent Minister*, Edwards similarly remarked: "Now death has veiled and hid from sight, a Star that shone with reflected light, our text and doctrine leads you to the Sun, that hath light in himself."[14]

Thus, the traditional cast of much of Edwards' thinking should not be overlooked. Tradition, at least as he interpreted it, was an important psychological factor in his own quest for regenerate selfhood. In his view tradition lies at the heart of history, and history is an allegory of the soul's spiritual progress. The soul or self figures very strongly in both *Distinguishing Marks* and *Some Thoughts*. In the latter Edwards speaks of the pitfalls lying before the pilgrim self, of which the principal two are worldly-mindedness and spiritual pride. Pride is the worse of the two because it remains "the last thing in a sinner that is overborn[e] by conviction, in order to conversion." Just as love is the chief of the affections, pride is the root of all sin. Edwards well knew from his own life how self-confidence could be the most secret of sins: "the heart is so deceitful and unsearchable in nothing in the world, as it is in this matter." Attempting to divest oneself from the layers of self-love is most frustrating because they "encompass the heart like the coats of an onion; if you pull off one, there is another underneath."

Humility is, of course, the key to the regenerate self. In the saint, Edwards explains in the earlier of the two works, "natural self-love" finally yields to "self-diffidence, self-emptiness, self-renunciation, and poverty of spirit." Humility will "annihilate self"; it is, we are told in *Some Thoughts*, the virtue which "makes a person like a little child, harmless and innocent." Paradoxically the saint can now discover true identity, a selfhood derived from divine parentage and defined in terms of a "resignation to the holy will of God." Aligned with the reality of the divine Self, the saint's love begins to transcend the narrow circle restricting the confused self searching for true identity, and, with expanding circumference, it starts to approach "an universal benevolence to mankind."

[14] *Works* (Austin), 8:409.

Love, therefore, is the principal affection of this new self, reflecting an image of divine Love.

IV. *With Steady and Constant Course*

Although both *Distinguishing Marks* and *Some Thoughts* influenced Edwards' contemporaries, a series of sermons he delivered during 1741–1742 and later revised as a book entitled *A Treatise Concerning Religious Affections* proved considerably more successful. It does not manifest the aesthetic qualities of several of his earlier works, but it is Edwards' summa on the nature of conversion as well as a remarkable specimen of lucid doctrinal writing. It reemphasizes a central point made in *Some Thoughts*: conversion is best studied in terms of its effects rather than its means. Among other things, such a notion suggests that the affections provide the most ascertainable index of these effects. While this focus on the affections led many of Edwards' contemporaries to place him entirely in the camp of the New Lights, a careful reading of *Religious Affections* will confirm the impression given by the preceding books that he was actually a moderate.

By the term *affections* Edwards means "the more vigorous and sensible exercises of the inclination and will of the soul," such as "fear, hope, love, hatred, desire, joy, sorrow, gratitude, compassion and zeal." They represent, in sum, "the spring of men's actions." That the affections are inseparable from the heart is a point Edwards made in *Some Thoughts* when he wrote: "All acts of the affections of the soul are in some sense acts of the will, and all acts of the will are acts of the affections." Similarly in *Religious Affections* he explains, "In some sense, the affection of the soul differs nothing at all from the will and inclination, and the will never is in any exercise any further than it is affected." This means, among other things, that the affections are expressions of the self.

If the will and the affections are thus joined, what of the other principal faculty of the soul? In answering this question Edwards once again confronted ideas with which he had wrestled in the preceding two books. In both *Distinguishing Marks* and *Some Thoughts*, he had refused to ignore the traditional view of reason

as the primary power of the soul and sought to forge a balance between the Old Lights' stress on this faculty and the New Lights'
concentration on emotion. *Religious Affections* reveals the same
irenic intention. Passages like the following one reiterate the traditional sequence with regard to the internal work of grace in the
soul: "a spiritual application of the promises of Scripture, for the
comfort of the saints, consists in enlightening their minds . . . ; thus
drawing forth their hearts to embrace the promiser, and the thing
promised; and by this means, giving the sensible actings of grace."
Reason is essential to Edwards' interpretation of the inner order of
the soul, but it does not dominate or usurp the will and affections.
Although in earlier works he had touched on the ticklish problem
of whether or not the enlightenment of reason necessarily precedes
the turning of the heart, he now fashioned a still broader compro-
mise according to which the faculties operate nearly simultaneously and, consequently, cannot be meaningfully differentiated in
their motions. Even in *Some Thoughts* he had suggested that the
understanding, albeit in a manner of speaking first of the components of the soul, should not be thought of as a power separate from
the affections, any more than should the will: "All affections are
raised either by light in the understanding, or by some error and
delusion in the understanding." "Holy affections are not heat without light," he explained further in *Religious Affections*, "but ever-
more arise from some information of the understanding, some
spiritual instruction that the mind receives, some light or actual
knowledge." If reason is as bound to the affections as is the heart,
then the understanding and the will must likewise be united. Indeed, Edwards alerted his readers to the error of speaking of these
two powers "as acting distinctly and separately."

Edwards' argument for the interrelatedness of the faculties
was not, in its broadest sense, original. Nevertheless, whether by
intent or by chance, his reassertion of this idea was a logical development from his repudiation of the notion that there were rigidly
prescribed stages preceding the reception of grace. By focusing on
the inseparableness of the faculties, Edwards reclaimed the mystery of conversion (as dramatized in the "Personal Narrative")
and at the same time bridged a major difference between the Old

and the New Lights. He allowed reason its technical primacy in the operation of the soul, but also argued for the soundness and importance of the affections in the drama of conversion.

Still another problem reared its head: what sort of rationality was involved? Actually, as early as *A Divine and Supernatural Light*, published in 1734, Edwards had suggested an answer to this question in his differentiation between common and special grace. In *Religious Affections*, however, he treats the subject in explicit detail. First he distinguishes between two kinds of knowledge. There is, on the one hand, "notional understanding" or "speculative knowledge." Basically dependent upon the sensorium, in Lockean terms, this knowledge concerns the facts of the material world in which man lives. On the other hand, there is "sensible" or "spiritual" knowledge, which is of a higher order than notional understanding and which is a product of the illumination of the intellect resulting a posteriori from special grace. This superior knowledge includes "the sense of the heart, wherein the mind don't only speculate and behold, but relishes and feels." In order to explain what he means, Edwards again resorts to the honey image he had used in *A Divine and Supernatural Light*: "he that has perceived the sweet taste of honey, knows much more about it, then he who has only looked upon and felt of it." Despite the Lockean aspect of this image, it is clear that reality is internally perceived. The very sense most crucial to the saint exists within. For Edwards, as we have observed earlier, what the inner senses detect in the terrain of the saint's heart reveals more of divine reality than does the interaction between the physical senses of the body and the exterior world.

In fact, Edwards' denunciation of the reliability of the physical senses emphasizes further that, next to Scripture, the gracious self provides the best revelation of divine reality. Warning of their deceptiveness, he explains: "the devil can't produce thoughts in the soul immediately, or any other way than by the animal spirits, or by the body; . . . he never brings to pass anything in the soul, but by the imagination or phantasy, or by exciting external ideas. For we know that alterations in the body, do immediately excite no other sort of ideas in the mind, but external ideas, or ideas of the outward senses, or ideas which are of the same outward nature."

For Edwards nature does not represent the source of deception; rather, the failure of human reason to regulate the senses properly and man's consequent disfranchisement from the essential beauty and harmony reflected in nature account for the problem. In Edwards' view, as a result, the psychic landscape of the self becomes more vitally informative to the saint than does the external world, for the inner senses are less easily deceived. This conclusion applies as well to practical piety; although outward expressions of piety are to be encouraged, "what is inward is of greatest importance."

New Lights no doubt read Edwards' designation of the important but secondary nature of good works in relation to the internal workings of the soul as a defense of their position. For many of the New Lights the soul's inner experience was all-sufficient, whereas for many of the Old Lights the performance of good works offered the best means of preparing for grace as well as disclosing one's spiritual state. Edwards' treatment of this question was a logical corollary to his notions about the self, with the consequence that it represents a more subtle position than one might first suspect. Similarly to his remarks on the role of reason in conversion, Edwards sought to bridge the two extreme attitudes toward practical piety. He realized that just as the faculties of the soul are united in their motions, so are the spiritual and the practical exercises of these faculties. He agreed with the Old Lights that one's earthly behavior in some way reflects the state of his soul; yet, he contended, "the main thing in this holy practice, is the holy acts of the mind, directing and governing the motions of the body." There is, in other words, a relation between the two akin to the one existing among reason, will, and affections. However, just as it is deceptive to speak of the faculties of the soul as separate principles, so is it erroneous to treat "Christian experience and practice, as if they were two things, properly and entirely distinct." The experience of grace in the soul and the practical exercises of the body are functionally indistinct: "spiritual practice in man, is the practice of a spirit and body jointly, or the practice of a spirit, animating, commanding and actualizing a body, to which it is united, and over which it has power." Good works are important only in conjunction with the actual turning of the heart.[15]

15 See *Works* (Dwight), 6:411.

Religious Affections represents one more testament to Edwards' view that the heart is the center of the drama of conversion and thereby the saint's most vital link to the reality of God. The unregenerate self, in contrast, renounces this connection to its very groundwork and, as a result, creates a mental gap between itself and God. With pride as its foundation the sinful soul "appears at a great distance" from God. For the saint, on the contrary, this gap is narrowed in direct proportion to the subjugation of pride. The more he is able, for instance, to avoid looking upon grace as a "*bonum utile*, a profitable good to me, that which greatly serves my interest, and so suits my self-love," and to acknowledge it as a "*bonum formosum*, a beautiful good in itself," the closer he gets to God. This alignment with God's perspective humbles the saints until they are disposed "to go to God, as children to a father, and behave towards God as children."

True love, as distinct from self-love, provides the key to the saint's alignment with God's Will. The entire self of the saint—reason, will, affections—becomes suffused with love "intuitively," for "love is the spirit of adoption, of the childlike principle." Love establishes the foundation for all the other affections. In his notebook Edwards wrote, "Love is certainly the perfection as well as the happiness of a spirit." This is so, he explained on another occasion, because God—"an ocean of love without shore or bottom"—conveys to the convert something of this divine excellency, which "changes the soul into an image of God's glory." Love metamorphoses the self into a luminary reflecting divine light, for the saint's "soul shall be as full of love as it shall be of light":[16]

> Grace in the soul is as much from Christ, as the light in a glass, held out in the sunbeams, is from the sun. But this represents the manner of the communication of grace to the soul, but in part; because the glass remains as it was, the nature of it not being changed, it is as much without any lightsomeness in its nature as ever. But the soul of a saint receives light from the Sun of Righteousness, in such a manner, that its nature is changed, and it becomes properly a luminous thing: not only does the sun shine in

---

[16] Untitled sermon on Rom. 2:10 (1740), in *Works* (Dwight), 8:231, 228, 268. The notebook entry may be found in *The Philosophy of Jonathan Edwards*, p. 258.

the saints, but they also become little suns, partaking of the nature of the fountain of their light.

The grace communicated to the saint is in some respect conveyed back to God: "The saints' love to God, is the fruit of God's love to them." Since the soul or self serves as the nexus of this mutual communication, it is there that Edwards finds God most intimately revealed. Predictably, then, he stresses introspection. "True religion disposes persons to be much alone, in solitary places," because the saint introspectively surveys the terrain of the heart in quest for the inner light revealing God's communication to him. Only by this light, he suggests in "The Peace Which Christ Gives His True Followers," are the saints' eyes opened, enabling them to see things as they are, and "the more they consider, and the more they know of the truth and reality of things, the more they know what is true concerning themselves, the state and condition they are in; the more they know of God." Clearly instrumental to this knowledge is the inner self where the reflected light "that they see things in" steadily grows "the brighter and the more searching."[17]

As Edwards had indicated in the "Personal Narrative" and *Some Thoughts*, the examination of the self is never fully resolved. In spite of some inward illumination the heart remains at best a foggy landscape, and the saint's introspective, rational eye cannot penetrate God's inscrutable ways. Although assurance is "attainable in some very extraordinary cases," the saint must generally eschew certainty while simultaneously maintaining a constant hope in his salvation. In December, 1740, Edwards had remarked that "the saints cannot always take comfort, and do not always taste the sweetness that there is in store for them, by reason of the darkness and clouds that sometimes interpose."[18] This notion, underlying the technique of the "Personal Narrative," corresponds to Edwards' conviction that there are no necessarily fixed, comprehendable steps in the conversion process. In *Religious Affections*, therefore, he concluded that "no order or method of operations and experiences, is any certain sign." The Holy Spirit is so "exceeding various in the manner of his operating, that in many cases it is impossible to trace him, or find out his way."

17 *Works* (Austin), 8:241.
18 Untitled sermon on Rom. 2:10, in *Works* (Dwight), 8:232.

Nevertheless, he contended, the Spirit often does give certain a posteriori signs, especially by means of the affective responses of the saint's whole being, soul and body. The affections provide clues to the spiritual condition of the soul because they are the expressions of reason and will, which is to say, of the self. Edwards presents twelve signs for assessing the spiritual state of the soul. Deriving much of his authority from such early divines as Thomas Shepard and William Ames, he incorporates the traditional stages of awakening, conviction, humiliation, and the turning of the heart in his discussion. He carefully transforms the formerly a priori linear sequence of these stages into generally indistinguishable a posteriori phases and refuses to have them understood as fixed criteria for determining who has special grace: "I am far from undertaking to give such signs of gracious affections, as shall be sufficient to enable any certainty to distinguish true affection from false in others." The trouble is that the external manifestations of the self, like the events of history, often appear to meander aimlessly, as if deprived of a focal center. This apparent characteristic obscures for man the divine scheme actually informing the soul's progress: "gracious affections are more a natural motion, like the stream of a river; which though it has many turns hither and thither, and may meet obstacles, and run more freely and swiftly in some places than others; yet in general, with a steady and constant course, tends the same way, till it gets to the ocean." There are no certain signs because the progress of the self cannot be fully mapped by man. What the "Personal Narrative" had dramatized is thus made explicit when Edwards agrees with Thomas Shepard that "sometimes the change made in a saint, at first work, is like a confused chaos; so that the saints know not what to make of it. The manner of the Spirit's proceeding in them that are born of the Spirit, is very often exceeding mysterious and unsearchable."

Men are not to despair in the face of this mystery. Everyone is duty-bound to search within himself. Since the self is, in conjunction with Scripture, the locus of God's revealing light, such introspection frequently provides evidence: "when they compare themselves with themselves, at different times, they may know, when grace is in lively exercise, that 'tis better with them than it was before." If so, they may well have detected a sign of spiritual growth, and, avoiding the bog of presumption, they may entertain "an assured hope of eternal life, while living here upon earth." This hope, in turn, generates a renewed fervor in one's quest for true spiritual identity; even though certainty, according to the divine plan, remains unattainable in most cases, nevertheless, "Christians are directed to give all dilligence to make their calling and election sure."

Although its conclusions were adumbrated in his previous writings, *Religious Affections* embodies Edwards' fullest statement about conversion. The book manifests a clarity and a tone intimating that it was for its author as much a personal as a public document. The best qualities in the book derive from the author's sense of judicious confidence. Over the years he had wrestled with the question of his own spiritual condition; he had probed, scrutinized, and forged whatever insight he had attained into public expositions. At times he may have felt that much of this activity, indeed his very life, seemed to lack a cohesive center. By the time he had written *Religious Affections*, however, he may well have had a clearer view of the underlying pattern of his life and work. This is a surmise, of course, but one deduced from the quality of writing, the tone and texture, of *Religious Affections*. As a participant in the greatest revival New England had ever witnessed (despite its excesses), Edwards must have felt closely aligned with the collective self of Puritanism and, consequently, with the divine Will informing its traditions. The insights expressed in his work might have struck him as bearing directly on New England's future history, especially in light of his belief that the truths discovered in the gracious inner self were inseparable from those revealed by the collective self of Puritan tradition. *Religious Affections* becomes, then, not merely an effort at compromising the antinomian and Arminian leanings of the more extreme members of the New and the Old Lights; it also expresses a personal testament of a heart hopefully in touch with the reality defined by the divine Self.

V. *Inward Exercises of the Mind*

During the years from 1744 to 1748, much of the fervor of the revival in Northampton again abated, and there were no new applications for church membership. Although the Awakening was still underway in other parts of New England, it is clear that when *Religious Affections* was published in 1746 the times were no longer propitious for its message. Besides the general spiritual malaise in his community, Edwards had been encountering difficulties of another sort. In 1742 there had been a painful dispute over his salary; in 1744 he had provoked an ill response from many parishioners as a result of his poor handling of an investigation of children who had secreted and read a book on midwifery; and in 1747 he suffered a personal loss when David Brainerd, missionary to the Indians and fiancé of his daughter, Jerusha, died of tuberculosis in his home. Jerusha, who had tended Brainerd during his illness, died shortly thereafter at the age of seventeen, and four months later Edwards' loyal friend, Colonel John Stoddard, passed away. These events no doubt reinforced Edwards' disposition toward introspection.

In 1749 he edited *An Account of the Life of the Late Reverend Mr. David Brainerd, Minister of the Gospel, Missionary to the Indians*. Edwards' motivation for editing Brainerd's diary partially stemmed from a desire to make good use of a document which provided further evidence for the arguments he had made earlier concerning conversion. The book also touched on other matters of interest to him, such as the distinction between enthusiastic and experimental religion as well as the indispensability of a learned ministry. A still more deeply personal level of motivation is suggested by the similarity between Brainerd's diary and that of Edwards. Edwards saw Brainerd's experience as a duplicate of his own, and the memoirs express Edwards' growing inner certitude about the nature of his insights concerning himself and the conversion experience. A further exploration of his own inner terrain, the book is suffused with a sense of affirmation, of an identity established. What Edwards found in the diary was confirmation of truths he had discovered during his own inward searches. Such identification was strengthened by the possibility that Providence had guided Brainerd to the Edwards household and moved him, through Edwards' persuasion, not to destroy his private papers, over which the older divine was now the appointed guardian. For a man who believed that every event, no matter how trivial on the surface, contributed to the unfolding of God's design for creation, there could be little doubt that this too was a sign. How could Edwards have escaped the conclusion that God intended that he should make public these papers, revelations derived from an inner self aligned with the divine Self? That he should be their editor was perfectly natural since they supported his own convictions that the inner self of the saint reveals divine truth. Indeed his role as editor would be identical to that of the controlling narrator in the "Personal Narrative." By disclosing the truth revealed by such an exploration of the inner self, Edwards would be contributing still further to the collective self of Puritan tradition, for it was clear to him that such examples are "set forth to public view" as a result of "the course of divine providence."[19]

Bypassing Brainerd's melancholy disposition and his excessive labors, Edwards focuses on how the young missionary "most accurately distinguished between real, solid piety, and enthusiasm; between those affections that are rational and scriptural—having their foundation in light and judgment—and those that are founded in whimsical conceits, strong impressions on the imagination, and vehement emotions of the animal spirits." Surely one fact of the Providential design behind the publication of this diary was the need to counter the "intemperate, imprudent zeal" which had characterized much of the revival. Edwards' use of the word *imprudent* is significant, especially when it is recalled that in *Distinguishing Marks* he had warned the Old Lights of an overemphasis on prudence. The conservative orientation of his moderate stance was even more pronounced during the waning years of the Awakening, when it seemed clearer to him that "neither people nor ministers had learned thoroughly to distinguish between solid religion and its delusive counterfeits. Even many ministers of the gospel, of long standing and the best reputation, were for a time overpowered with the glaring appearances of the latter." Such a remark is bifocal. In part it seeks to exonerate Brainerd from his youthful intemperance and enthusiasm; in another sense it ex-

[19] This work and the two previously published portions of Brainerd's journal appear in Edwards, *Memoirs of the Rev. David Brainerd; Missionary to the Indians on the Borders of New-York, New-Jersey, and Pennsylvania: Chiefly Taken from His Own Diary. By Rev. Jonathan Edwards, of Northampton* (New Haven, 1822). This volume should be used with caution because it is not faithful to Edwards' original publication.

presses Edwards' own sense of guilt. Edwards had never, as we have seen, endorsed the excessive aspects of the revival, so in this comment he is not repudiating his own efforts during those times. But by 1749 the reactionary train of his thoughts, stimulated by the postrevival problems now surfacing in Northampton, particularly nurtured his basic traditional allegiances. A suggestion of how distrustful he felt about the later phases of the Awakening is unveiled in his insistence that Brainerd's "course of religion began *before* the late times of extraordinary religious commotion" (Edwards' italics), a comment made at least twice in the *Account*.

Also of interest is his observation on the missionary's conversion experience. Although Edwards was aware from his own inner probings as well as from what he had witnessed in others that the drama of conversion did not necessarily conform to the sort of a priori steps delineated by some of the earlier divines, the *Account* reveals his continuing interest in the subject raised so long ago in his diary and, perhaps, a lingering unconscious anxiety over the matter. His explanation for mentioning the subject—to foreclose on any objections, based on the older system, to Brainerd's sainthood—fails to cloak the element of latent inner tension concerning an issue which had occupied his mind to a significant extent for nearly twenty-six years:

> I am far from thinking, and so was he, that clearness in the order of experiences is, in any measure, of equal importance with the clearness of their nature. I have sufficiently declared in my discourse on religious affections, which he expressly approved of and recommended, that I do not suppose, a sensible distinctness of the steps of the Spirit's operation and method of successive convictions and illuminations, is a necessary requisite to persons being received in full charity, as true saints; provided the nature of the things which they profess be right, and their practice correspondent. Nevertheless, it is observable,—a fact which cuts off all objection from such as would be most unreasonably disposed to object and cavil in the present case,—that Brainerd's experiences were not only clear in the latter respect, but remarkably so in the former.

Thus, Brainerd's conversion arose from "immediate divine influence, supernaturally enlightening and convincing the mind, and powerfully impressing, quickening, sanctifying, and governing the heart." The sequence is significant. Brainerd's own words often read as if they were drawn from a case study intended for *Religious Affections*, as in the following instance: "unspeakable glory seemed to open to the view and apprehension of my soul. I do not mean any external brightness, for I saw no such thing; nor do I intend any imagination of a body of light, some where in the third heavens, or any thing of that nature; but it was a new inward apprehension or view that I had of God, such as I never had before, nor any thing which had the least resemblance of it. I stood still; wondered; and admired!" It is no wonder that Edwards pruned the diary less than he might have; it confirmed his own impressions. It too, like the "Personal Narrative," dramatized how grace, not necessarily operating in a precise, linear sequence of stages, always engaged the totality of one's being. Because this moment of the immediate indwelling of the Holy Spirit is so elusive that His very presence can be espied only in the retrospective light of the entire range of the self's experiences, Edwards felt obliged to present an only slightly edited version of Brainerd's self-portrait.

The self, of course, is central to the *Account*, the theme of which is "the wonderful change [Brainerd] experienced in his mind and disposition." In his youth Brainerd was, like Edwards, at first unable to accept the idea of God's absolute sovereignty. He was reluctant to "relinquish all self-confidence," which meant that he had to contend with "spiritual pride and self-exaltation," even "self-worship." This problem was eventually overcome, and Brainerd gradually realized, as he explained in his prefatory remarks to Thomas Shepard's meditations, that "Self-Emptiness, Self-Loathing" and a deep, unfeigned "Self-Abasement" are characteristics of the true saint.[20] For Brainerd, as for Edwards, the self represents the key to one's identity. Identity depends on the quality of the love and humility in the heart. Self-love per se emerges from false identity; self-love is permissible, as Edwards explained in *Religious Affections*, only when it is put into proper perspective—that is, only when the self, aligned to the divine Will through genuine love, possesses true identity. Brainerd seems to agree with Edwards' view when he writes: "when a soul loves God with a su-

20 *Three Valuable Pieces*, ed. Thomas Prince, p. v.

preme love, he therein acts like the blessed God himself, who most justly loves himself in that manner. So when God's interest and his are become one, and he longs that God should be glorified, and rejoices to think he is unchangeably possessed of the highest glory and blessedness, herein also he acts in conformity to God." This comment represents Brainerd's equivalent to Edwards' use of the luminary image to describe the soul's relation to the divine Self. That Edwards was particularly sensitive to this passage is evident from the fact that he specifically cites it in *True Saints, When Absent from the Body, Are Present with the Lord*, the sermon he preached at Brainerd's funeral (October 12, 1747).

Just how faithful to the original is Edwards' account of the memoirs must remain a matter of speculation since Brainerd's manuscripts are no longer extant. I think we can dismiss any serious qualms about deliberate falsifications, such matters as additions or deletions that would (in his opinion, at least) substantially alter the meaning of the journals. On the other hand, we might well caution ourselves about too readily assuming that he, as an editor, deleted only trivial items. He frankly announces that the book is "chiefly taken" from the diaries and that some parts have been "left out for brevity's sake." On the whole he is quite reluctant to repeat what Brainerd had published from his journals in *Mirabilia Dei inter Indicos* (1746) and in *Divine Grace Displayed* (1746). Moreover, he particularly ignores the missionary's external activities. This is reasonable when understood in terms of Edwards' purpose to present "the inward exercises of [Brainerd's] mind." There is, however, an intriguing possibility, to be discussed shortly, that some of Edwards' deletions may have been motivated by his view of the Lord's Supper.

VI. *The Ways of Our Fathers*

In the same year in which the *Account* appeared, Edwards published *An Humble Inquiry into the Rules of the Word of God Concerning the Qualifications Requisite to a Compleat Standing and Full Communion in the Visible Christian Church*. In the Preface to this work he explains, "I have the same opinion concerning the religion and inward experiences chiefly in vogue among them [the enthusiasts], as I had when I wrote my *Treatise on Religious*

Affections, and when I wrote my *Observations and Reflections on Mr. Brainerd's Life*."[21] Many of the Northampton congregation felt otherwise and deemed their minister's opinions, as expressed in this new book, inconsistent with his former thinking and practice. At issue was the administration of the Lord's Supper.

Puritan custom, established sometime during the first decade of their settlement in New England, excluded the unconverted from this sacrament. This practice caused few problems initially because the controlling faction of the first generation was apparently largely made up of visible saints. Those seeking admission to the church and the sacraments were required to pass an examination of their religious knowledge and of their spiritual experience before the elders. They also had to answer whatever charges might be brought against them by other church members. If they were approved, then they were expected to make a "spiritual relation" on the day of their admission. Requiring this profession became a standard practice.

As the years passed, the succeeding generations did not inherit the religious ardor of their parents and were less inclined to present themselves for church membership. Then too the town populations increased as a result of subsequent emigrations from Europe, and these new citizens had not emigrated to the colony because of the same strong religious sentiment which had motivated its founders. The Puritan church, consequently, found itself in a dilemma: on the one hand, it desired to preserve its purity; on the other hand, it wanted to maintain its authority in the community. One step toward resolving the problem was the institution of the Halfway Covenant by the Synod of 1662. This decision permitted the children of all baptised parents, whether or not these parents were full church members, to receive the sacrament of baptism. This procedure, it was reasoned, would place the children halfway into the church, thereby providing incentive for them to pursue admission to the Lord's Supper. The Halfway Covenant was not, however, instantly popular nor did it prove sufficient in curbing the decline of religion.

To some ministers it was becoming clear that if the church were to remain a real force in the lives of these former children

21 This tract is printed in *Works* (Austin), 1:145–335.

who were now adults, all technical barriers to membership might have to be eliminated. Solomon Stoddard, Edwards' grandfather, saw the need for further liberality and began the practice of open communion in Northampton sometime between 1677 and 1690. This procedure, permitting all morally sincere Christians to receive the sacrament, stirred considerable controversy. Although not the first to practice open communion, Stoddard was a leading figure and, as such, the target of more than one polemic decrying the opening of the sacrament to the unregenerate.[22]

In the *Humble Inquiry* as well as *Misrepresentations Corrected, and Truth Vindicated* (an answer, published in 1752, to Solomon Williams' attack on the earlier book), Edwards sought to realign the observance of the Lord's Supper with the older tradition established by the first generation of New England Puritans. He did not intend to revive the custom of admission to church membership and then to the sacrament in its strictest terms, but he was certainly calling for a halt to the current practice in Northampton. By way of introduction to this touchy matter, he cited his grandfather's words: "It may possibly be a fault (says Mr. Stoddard) to depart from the ways of our fathers: But it may also be a virtue, and an eminent act of obedience, to depart from them in some things." This was, in a sense, a brilliant maneuver, since it gave Edwards support for his position from his grandfather's work, an authority derived from the very man whose practice Edwards was trying to controvert. The passage made clear, in Stoddard's own words, that the institution of open communion in Northampton was indeed a departure from older custom and may in actuality have been a mistake. Edwards had the advantage; in essence, he simultaneously claimed the authority of "father" Stoddard as well as that of the fathers of the first generation. The subtlety of Edwards' procedure was completely wasted on his opponents, who were not about to abdicate their "rights" to open communion.

In *An Humble Inquiry* Edwards, who assisted Stoddard in

[22] See Perry Miller, "Solomon Stoddard, 1643–1729," *Harvard Theological Review* 34 (October 1941): 277–320; Thomas Schafer, "Solomon Stoddard and the Theology of the Revival," in *A Miscellany of American Christianity*, pp. 328–361; James P. Walsh, "Solomon Stoddard's Open Communion: A Reexamination," *New England Quarterly* 43 (March 1970): 97–114; and E. Brooks Holifield, *The Covenant Sealed*.

Northampton for two years, makes clear that the real issue lay in his grandfather's understanding of the expression "visible saints." In Stoddard's opinion, a distinction should be made between true and visible sainthood. He interpreted the expression *visible saints* to apply to those who are morally sincere, many of whom he readily admitted are "hippocrites" lacking "a thorow work of conversion." "When such profess faith," Stoddard explained, "they make a true Profession, they profess that which they do indeed believe, though their profession be not graciously sincere . . . though they only do it with a moral, and not with a gracious sincerity."[23] Stoddard's thought reflects Presbyterian influences; it reasserts Saint Augustine's distinction between the pure invisible church and the imperfect visible one, without equally taking into account this church father's stress on purifying the visible church.

Stoddard further defined the difference in terms of two covenants, an external one for those who have only common grace (visible saints) and an internal one for those who have special or saving grace (true saints). His reasoning led him to take a wider view of the Lord's Supper. In his opinion members of the external covenant as well as those of the internal covenant had a right to the seals of this sacrament. Contrary to more orthodox interpretation, he asserted that the sacrament was not the seal of one's faith or salvation but of one's covenant relation. He thus concluded that "Sanctifying grace is not necessary in order to a lawful attending the Lords-Supper." He admitted that the sacrament was to be reserved only "for Church Members and not for other men," by which he meant that he limited it only to visible saints. But, as we noted, his failure to differentiate between the expressions *church members* and *visible saints* violated the general understanding of these words by an earlier Puritan establishment. Stoddard had in effect opened the sacrament to anyone who was morally sincere at the simplest level. His prerequisite of baptism, as he himself knew, in no way prevented the unregenerate from partaking of the Lord's Supper.

Edwards had been uncomfortable with this practice for some time, and in 1748 he attempted to reestablish the more traditional understanding of church membership. In *An Humble Inquiry* he

---

[23] *An Appeal to the Learned*, pp. 16, 17.

rejects the distinction Stoddard made between visible and true saints, explaining that the expression *visible saints* refers to those "who give probable appearances of holiness" rather than to those who are merely morally sincere. Claiming that there is but one covenant, he dismisses the notion of speculative or doctrinal knowledge, which arises from common grace, as providing any valid justification for church membership. Visible saints are those who possess an intuitive or experiential knowledge, those who are "immediately concerned." They not only rationally assent but willingly consent to God. Their covenant is a marriage, Edwards explains, resorting to a traditional image. The saints are married to Christ, and the contract must not be entered into half-heartedly by either party: "the visible transaction, or mutual profession there is between Christ and the visible church, is abundantly compared to the mutual profession there is in marriage. In marriage the bride professes to yield to the bridegroom's suit, and to take him for her husband, renouncing all others, and to give up herself to him to be entirely and forever possessed by him as his wife." This means, for Edwards, that either one is or is not married to Christ, that there cannot be two covenants as Stoddard had delineated. The "practice of promiscuous admission" to the Lord's Supper, it follows, violates the celebration of this marriage contract.

Edwards' traditionalist line of thought leads him to reaffirm that this sacrament is not a converting ordinance. The Lord's Supper, he explains, is a seal of the covenant of grace or the marriage of the soul to Christ. Consequently, it should be restricted to only those who appear to be among the elect. Nor does baptism properly designate who is a visible saint and therefore eligible to partake of the second sacrament: "All that acknowledge infant baptism, allow infants, who are the proper subjects of baptism, and are baptized, to be in some sort members of the Christian Church; yet none suppose them to be members in such standing as to be the proper immediate subjects of all ecclesiastical ordinances and privileges: But that some further qualifications are requisite in order to this, to be obtained, either in a course of nature, or by education, or by divine grace." Edwards was underscoring the significance of baptism as set forth by the Halfway Covenant. But his increasing traditionality in ecclesiastical practice made him uncertain even of this practice, for elsewhere in *An Humble Inquiry* he suggested the still more unpopular position that perhaps baptism should be administered only to visible saints (in his strict interpretation of the term) and their children. There is a hint of Edwards' distrust of the Halfway Covenant, which was designed to admit to baptism the children of all Christian parents. Edwards' sensitivity to this issue is related to his recurrent complaint about the dissolution of family order. Such a restriction on baptism, he reasoned, would make parents more anxious over the spiritual welfare of their children and so incline them to seek full membership in the church for themselves as well as for their progeny. Later, at Stockbridge, the cast of Edwards' conservatism would deepen, and he would refuse to administer baptism merely upon request.

In order to determine, as best as he could, who were the visible saints, Edwards attempted to restore the spiritual relation as the prerequisite to admission to the Lord's Supper. He never suggested, however, such a profession was necessary for the approval of fellow members. In *Some Thoughts* he had warned that "God seems so strictly to have forbidden this practice of our judging our brethren in the visible church, not only because he knew that we were too much of babes, infinitely too weak, fallible and blind, to be well capacitated for it, but also because he knew that it was not a work suited to our proud hearts; that it would be setting us vastly too high, and making us too much of lords over our fellow creatures." This caution was similarly expressed in *Distinguishing Marks*, when Edwards explained the inconsistency of maintaining "that men have ability and right to determine the state of the souls of visible Christians": "it supposes that God has given men power to make another visible church within his visible church; for by visible Christians or those that are of God's visible church, can be understood nothing else than that company that are Christians or saints, *visibly so*; i.e. that have a right to be received as such in the eye of a public charity." Although in these passages Edwards explicitly addressed problems concerning the evaluation of the spiritual state of those already *within* the visible church, his emphasis on the inscrutableness of a man's interior was central to his notion of admission to church membership. He readily admitted, as he wrote in *Religious Affections*, that such matters could not be determined with certitude, that "judging what is in men by outward appearances, is at best uncertain, and liable to deceit," and that "when there are many probable appearances of piety in others, it is the duty of the saints to receive them cordially into their charity, and to love them and rejoice in them, as their brethren in Christ Jesus." Even he, as a minister, may not act in certitude but only in an advisory fashion, as he observed in *An Humble Inquiry*: "the pastor is not to act as a searcher of the heart, or a lord of conscience in this affair, yet that hinders not but that he may and ought to inquire particularly into the experiences of the souls committed to his care and charge, that he may be under the best advantages to instruct and advise them, to apply the teachings and rules of God's word unto them, for their selfexamination, to be helpers of their joy, and promoters of their salvation."

What principally motivated Edwards' affirmation of the spiritual relation was less his desire to secure a firmer grasp over his communal family or his predilection for Puritan tradition than his preoccupation with the self in the drama of conversion. Not intending it to serve as any means whereby others might measure someone's spiritual state, he hoped the relation would encourage selfexamination on the part of the petitioner. As he expressed the matter in a letter to the Reverend Peter Clark of Salem Village (May 7, 1750), what he objected to was a public "assenting to the form of words rehearsed on occasion of admission to the Communion" instead of a sincere "hearty consent to the Terms of the Gospel Covenant of Grace."[24] Merely to *assent* involves only the intellect, whereas to *consent* requires the will (Edwards' use of the word *hearty* is emphatically redundant). Genuine consent necessitates a thorough searching of the heart. Such introspection, as we have seen, had become very central to Edwards' thinking, especially as the gracious self loomed larger and larger as a source of divine revelation. Thus, admission to the sacrament, in his view, could hardly depend on the discretion of the minister or the visible saints but should stem from the pious, ardent resolve of the individual seeking membership. The spiritual relation only provided a vehicle for an attestation to this resolution arising from an earnest

[24] George Peirce Clark, "An Unpublished Letter by Jonathan Edwards," *New England Quarterly* 29 (June 1956): 228–233.

encounter with the inner self and the sense of genuine faith discovered there.

Edwards readily conceded that the profession did not have to conform to any specific formula. To be sure, he had written in *Religious Affections*, " 'tis not necessary they should give an account of the particular steps and method, by which the Holy Spirit, sensibly to them, wrought and brought about those great essential things of Christianity in their hearts." But a sincere spiritual relation, based on self-scrutiny, is paramount, if the sanctity of the Lord's Supper is to be preserved. Edwards did not want the sacrament taken for granted any more than he wanted church membership to be. Having witnessed the complacency that resulted from the more liberal practice of his grandfather, Edwards sought to restore man's incentive to spiritual improvement. A genuine profession of faith, in contrast to Stoddard's relaxed practice, would require each applicant to engage in a thorough inward searching of the self, thereby providing clues to his spiritual condition.

Significantly, on the title page of *An Humble Inquiry* Edwards cited a double-edged quotation from Job: "Behold now I have opened my Mouth:—My Words shall be of the Uprightness of my Heart." This passage announces that *An Humble Inquiry* is for Edwards a profession of doctrine derived from the deep introspection of his own heart, which he hoped mirrored something of divine revelation. Later, in the *Farewel-Sermon*, he would remark concerning his position on the Lord's Supper, that he could not remain silent, "being satisfied what his [God's] will was, after a long, diligent, impartial, and prayerful, inquiry."[25] The passage from Job at the same time also defines, with the authority of Scripture, the validity of the spiritual relation; each Christian was likewise to give expression to what he discerns of the Spirit's work in his soul. In Edwards' opinion, then, the Lord's Supper should be reserved for those alone who could thank God for a sincere hope in their salvation, an expressible hope engendered by the exploration of the inner self.

In the light of these remarks we may, I think, raise questions about Edwards' editing of Brainerd's memoirs. In his prefatory re-

[25] *Works* (Austin), 1:127.

marks to *An Humble Inquiry,* he acknowledges that the opinions he is about to set forth are the same that he held while writing *Religious Affections* and the *Account,* adding the specific comment, "I was of the same mind concerning the qualifications of communicants at the Lord's Table, that I am of now." This remark becomes doubly significant when it is juxtaposed to another appearing in the *Account,* in which Edwards speaks of Brainerd's Indian saints: "I never supposed, every one of those Indians, who in profession, renounced their Heathenism and visibly embraced Christianity, and have had some appearance of piety, will finally prove true converts." These remarks may suggest a covert motive behind Edwards' reluctance to report in the *Account* the substance of Brainerd's printed journals. Although he claims to have deleted whatever of the journals had been previously printed, a careful comparison of these documents reveals that Edwards is rather selective in his editing. Not everything appearing in the published journals has actually been deleted from the *Account,* and, frequently, what has been excluded is done so at the expense of the reader, who sometimes requires the excised details in order to comprehend certain subsequent events and observations. Our suspicions are further sustained by Edwards' admission to having omitted "that which in some Respects is the most remarkable, and to a Christian Mind would be the most pleasant Part of the whole Story," namely Brainerd's "greatest Success, in his Labours for the good of Souls, and in his particular Business as a Missionary to the Indians."[26]

My surmise is that Edwards may in fact have disapproved of or at least felt discomfort over the missionary's report on the Indians' emotional response to religion and on their celebration of the Lord's Supper. To present these matters as part of his portrait of Brainerd's exemplary life would not help ameliorate the state of affairs of the post-Awakening period. In spite of the fact that in the *Account* he asserted his trust in the young man's ability to differentiate between experimental and enthusiastic religion, Edwards surely must have paused over such a passage as the following from *Mirabilia Dei inter Indicos*: "The cry of these was soon heard by

---

[26] For these passages see the first edition of the *Account* (Boston 1749), pp. 156–157.

others, who, though scattered before, immediately gathered round. I then proceeded in the same strain of gospel-invitation, till they were all melted into tears and cries, except two or three."

If he harbored doubts about the most remarkable part of the story—that is, the extent of Brainerd's success in finding true converts among the Indians—he must certainly have been reluctant to report much concerning the missionary's administration of the Lord's Supper to them. Brainerd was an ordained Presbyterian minister and seems to have been Stoddardean in his view of the sacrament. He was very familiar with Stoddard's teachings, especially *A Guide to Christ*. It is significant, I think, that the most central events in *Divine Grace Displayed*, the entries for April 25, 26, and 27, 1746, are entirely deleted from the *Account*. As it appears in the printed journal, the first entry includes the following statement: "Of late I apprehend that a number of persons in my congregation were proper subjects of the ordinance of the Lord's Supper, and that it might be seasonable speedily to administer it to them; and having taken advice of some of the reverend correspondents in this solemn affair; I accordingly proposed and appointed the next Lord's day, with leave of divine providence, for the administration of this ordinance." Edwards, to be sure, would have approved of Brainerd's conscientiousness in seeking advice in the matter, but he may well have doubted the wisdom of the decision. Nowhere in the *Account* does he refer to the missionary's first administration of the sacrament to twenty-three Indians. Other remarks included in Brainerd's diary may provide clues to Edwards' editorial silence: "I catechised those who were designed to partake of the Lord's supper the next day . . . and had abundant satisfaction respecting their doctrinal knowledge and fitness in that respect for an attendance upon it"; "I have abundant reason to think, that those who came to the Lord's table had a good degree of doctrinal knowledge of the nature and design of the ordinance, and that they acted with understanding in what they did." For Brainerd, doctrinal knowledge and moral sincerity were apparently sufficient criteria for admission to the sacrament. He does not mention that the Indians ever gave any evidence of the work of the Holy Spirit in their hearts. We may suspect, for reasons expressed in *An Humble Inquiry*, that Edwards did not altogether approve of Brainerd's practice of open admission to the Lord's Supper and, as well, that this dubiety was influential in his editing of the missionary's memoirs.

Yet nothing we have noted accuses Edwards of deception. He could not have deliberately falsified the document and still have seen it as a contribution to the revelation of the divine Will. He could, nevertheless, in his own mind justify his silence and his deemphasis of Brainerd's "greatest Success," if he believed that doing so would further the unfolding of divine truth. He does not, we should observe, evade the issue completely. Later in the *Account*, in an entry dated June 8, 1746, he mentions Brainerd's administration of the sacrament to the Indians; it simply reads: "A Number of my dear People sat down by themselves at the last Table; at which Time God seem'd to be in the midst of them."[27] The reader is never told when the missionary commenced this practice; the event is merely included as a peripheral detail subsumed in the overall narration of Brainerd's life. Comparison with the ebullient original entry indicates the degree to which Edwards' presentation of the event departs from that of Brainerd:

> Most of my people, who had been communicants at the Lord's table, before being present at this sacramental occasion, communed with others in the holy ordinance, at the desire, and I trust to the satisfaction and comfort of numbers of God's people, who had longed to see this day, and whose hearts had rejoiced in this work of grace among the Indians, which prepared the way for what appeared so agreeable at this time. Those of my people who communed, seemed in general, agreeably affected at the Lord's table, and some of them considerably melted with the love of Christ, although they were not so remarkably refreshed and feasted at this time, as when I administered this ordinance to them in our own congregation only. A number of my dear people sat down by themselves at the last table; at which time God seemed to be in the midst of them. Some of the by-standers were affected with seeing those who had been "aliens from the common wealth of Israel, and strangers to the covenant of promise" . . . now brought near to God, as his professing people, and sealing their covenant with him, by a solemn and devout attendance upon this sacred ordinance. As members of God's people were refreshed with this sight, and thereby excited to bless God for the enlarge-

27 Ibid., p. 188.

ment of his kingdom in the world; so some others, I was told, were awakened by it, apprehending the danger they were in of being themselves finally cast out; while they saw others from the east and west preparing, and hopefully prepared in some good measure, to sit down in the kingdom of God.

Other meager references to the admission of Indians to the sacrament subsequently appear in the *Account*, but not once do any of them elicit comment from Edwards. We never get a real glimpse of Brainerd's excitement over this stage of his ministerial relationship with the Indians or of its effect on "what passed in his own heart." It is reasonable, I think, to interpret Edwards' handling of this matter as an indication of how large the issue loomed in his mind. *An Humble Inquiry*, in short, seems to declare explicitly the motivations covertly informing his editorial silence in the *Account*.

The opening quotation from Job notwithstanding, *An Humble Inquiry* reveals an undercurrent of defensiveness. Edwards confessed, "I have formerly been of his [Stoddard's] opinion, which I imbibed from his books, even from my childhood, and have in my proceedings conformed to his practice; though never without some difficulties in my view, which I could not solve." After nearly twenty-three years of conformity to his grandfather's practice, he was now publicly reversing himself. In the same year, shortly before the appearance of the book, he commented in a letter to John Erskine how he no longer could conform to the current practice, adding, "I have had difficulties with respect to it, which have been long increasing; till I dared no longer to proceed in the former way; which has occasioned great uneasiness among my people, and has filled all the country with noise, which has obliged me to write something on the subject, which is now in the press. I know not but this affair will issue in a separation between me and my people."[28] Relying on the truths derived from his inner convictions rather than on the practical realities of the times, Edwards' attempt to return to the ways of the fathers was doomed. The comments in his letter to John Erskine would prove prophetic and he would soon find himself in exile.

28 Dwight, *Life of Edwards*, p. 276.

[5]

Virtue and Identity:
Last Works

IN 1750 a council was called to determine whether Edwards and the Northampton congregation could be reconciled. It decided by a majority of one vote that the minister should depart from his parish. Although Edwards had anticipated this outcome, the decision troubled him deeply. There is ample evidence that his dismissal weighed heavily on his mind throughout the remaining years of his life. He knew that, like everything else, this event was a sign from God; the trouble was, however, to determine whether God was displeased with the minister or with the parishioners of Northampton. He knew that most probably the congregation was at fault; yet did not his dismissal also point to his failure as well? In a letter dated July 1, 1751, he wrote: "I would be far from so laying all the blame of the sorrowful things that have come to pass, to the people, as to suppose that I have no cause of self-reflection and humiliation before God on this occasion. I am sensible that it becomes me to look on what has lately happened, as an awful frown of heaven on me, as well as on the people."[1] Once more he found himself searching his heart for some insight into the mysterious ways of God; for, as he had remarked in his diary as early as 1722 concerning such trials, "God intends when we meet with them, to desire us to look back on our ways."[2]

Ten days after his formal dismissal he delivered a sermon, later published as *A Farewel-Sermon Preached at the First Pre-*

[1] *The Great Awakening*, ed. C. C. Goen, pp. 564–565.
[2] Dwight, *Life of Edwards*, p. 77.

cinct in Northampton, After the People's Publick Rejection of Their Minister, and Renouncing Their Relation to Him as Pastor of the Church There. Actually this was not the final sermon he preached in the town. Northampton could not immediately secure a new pastor, nor could Edwards, now forty-six years of age, readily find a new position. As a result, he had an opportunity to deliver several sermons during this time, a situation which did not please his opponents. When rumors began to circulate that another meeting house might be constructed in order to accommodate him, Edwards became the subject of still more discussions. Eventually he accepted a post at Stockbridge, an Indian mission of the sort frequently left to laymen, where he would take on the role of prophet in exile.

I. *Of Shepherds and Flocks*

The *Farewel-Sermon* is more than a curiosity. It is a carefully, at times even subtly, written indictment of the people of Northampton. Yet it also reveals a genuine attempt on Edwards' part to be objective about his dismissal; he knew that "ministers, and the people that have been under their care, must meet one another before Christ's tribunal at the day of judgment."[3] On that "day of infallible decision, and of the everlasting and unalterable sentence," God would impartially declare who was right and who was mistaken. Then ministers "will give an account of the ill treatment of such as have not well received them and their messages from Christ"; then too congregations will "rise up in judgment against wicked and unfaithful ministers, who have sought their own temporal interest more than the good of the souls of their flock." Edwards seems willing to leave the matter in the hands of God.

This element of objectivity, however, is undercut by an apparent defensiveness, for there is more than one hint in the sermon that God's "unalterable sentence" and its resulting "everlasting separation" of a congregation from its minister may well constitute an eternal indictment of Edwards' adversaries. This indictment is particularly manifested by Edwards' references to the family throughout the work. We have already remarked Edwards' fascination with this image and how he relates it to the collective self of

[3] This sermon appears in *Works* (Austin), 1:101–141.

Puritan tradition, the continuity of which reveals something of the divine Will. It is, then, to be expected that he would resort to this image in defending his return to the more orthodox practice of closed communion.

The image of the family appears at the very beginning of the sermon: "We live in a world of change, where nothing is certain or stable; and where a little time, a few revolutions of the sun, bring to pass strange things, surprising alterations, in particular persons, in families, in towns and churches, in countries and nations." The progression of images in this comment moves from the individual to expanding rings of familial relations. It is in terms of this traditional datum, this principle of order remaining constant in the flux of time, that he construes his dismissal from Northampton. In other words, the *Farewel-Sermon* expresses a plea for "the maintaining of family order." Once more Edwards urges the fathers of the community to take charge of their respective families. "The due regulation of your families is of no less, and, in some respects, of much greater importance," he explains, "every Christian family ought to be as it were a little church, consecrated to Christ, and wholly influenced and governed by his rules. And family education and order are some of the chief of the means of grace."[4]

He had touched on this point in *Some Thoughts* when he remarked: "Every Christian family is a little church, and the heads of it are its authoritative teachers and governors." By the same token, the church should be like a family, in which the minister is the spiritual husband or father. Just as the bridelike soul of the saint is wedded to Christ, so too the members of the church are married to Christ's ministerial ambassador. In "The Church's Marriage to Her Sons, and to Her God," which he delivered at the installment of Samuel Buel at East Hampton, Edwards observed that "as the bridegroom and bride give themselves to each other in covenant; so it is in that union . . . between a faithful pastor and a Christian people."[5] The role of the congregation, therefore, is "to love and honor him, and willingly submit yourselves to him, as a

---

[4] The increased emphasis on the responsibility of the family in the New World to educate the young is discussed in Lawrence A. Cremin, *American Education.*

[5] *Works* (Austin), 8:313–350.

virgin when married to an husband"; "in rejecting him," Edwards warns, "you will reject Christ."

In the *Farewel-Sermon* Edwards emphasizes the minister's position as the spiritual father of the ecclesiastical family. He admonishes his former parishioners to consider "whether you have had from me the treatment which is due to spiritual children, and whether you have treated me as you ought to have treated a spiritual father." They are to attend to this question because, just "as the relation of a natural parent brings great obligations on children in the sight of God; so much more, in many respects, does the relation of a spiritual father bring great obligations upon such whose conversation [conversion] and eternal salvation they suppose God has made them the instruments of." Since a correspondence exists between the family and the church, comments touching on one necessarily imply the other. Thus when Edwards discusses the need for order in the actual families of Northampton, he also has in mind the more extensive rings of familial relations—especially the church and the state, both of which are superstructures founded on individual family units. The double entendre of the following remark provides a good illustration: "let children obey their parents, and yield to their instructions, and submit to their orders, as they would inherit a blessing and not a curse. For we have reason to think, from many things in the word of God, that nothing has a greater tendency to bring a curse on persons in this world, and on all their temporal concerns, than an undutiful, unsubmissive, disorderly behavior in children towards their parents." From Edwards's point of view, disobedient spiritual children rebelling against him threaten to bring disorder and a curse upon the ecclesiastical and the communal family of Northampton.

The family motif is subtly reinforced by references to shepherds and flocks. Edwards conventionally transfers these images from Christ to ministers, who must perform pastoral duties; such a transference effectively helps him score a psychological victory over his detractors. He begins by echoing the luminary image he associates with the clergy in *Resort and Remedy* and *True Excellency*, reminding his audience that ministers are "as lights set up in the churches" which reflect Christ's second coming when "all deceit and illusion shall vanish away before the light of that day."

Ministers are ambassadors whose function parallels that of the "chief Shepherd," a fact permitting Edwards to declare: "I have endeavored to do the part of a faithful shepherd, in feeding the lambs as well as the sheep." It is pertinent that in "parting with this flock," which was once under his "pastoral care," Edwards warns the congregation to be cautious in selecting a new minister, lest they ultimately discover themselves "exposed as sheep without a shepherd," a disorderly family without a spiritual father.

Not only did Edwards conclude the *Farewell-Sermon* with fatherly advice on the spiritual and secular welfare of the community, but nearly two years later he appended a letter to *Misrepresentations Corrected* in order to remind Northampton again about the necessity of maintaining proper parental example and family order. The image likewise informs a letter he wrote in 1750, in which he expressed a hope that God would show "a fatherly care" for him and his family now that they have been dismissed from Northampton; it occurs similarly in a letter he wrote in 1754 to Major Joseph Hawley, formerly one of his detractors; and it emerges centrally in his alleged deathbed comments to one of his daughters in 1758: "as to my children, you are now like to be left fatherless, which I hope will be an inducement to you all to seek a Father, who will never fail you."[6] That Edwards' reliance on this image is tantamount to his respect for tradition becomes particularly apparent in *An Humble Attempt to Promote Explicit Agreement and Visible Union of God's People in Extraordinary Prayer for the Revival of Religion and the Advancement of Christ's Kingdom on Earth* (1747), in which he complained of the present age, "wherein those mean and stingy principles (as they are called) of our forefathers, which (as is supposed) deformed religion . . . are very much discarded, and grown out of credit, and supposed more free, noble and generous thoughts of the nature of religion, and of the Christian scheme, are entertained; but yet never was an age, wherein religion in general was so much dispised and trampled

---

[6] The letter of 1750 appears in Dwight, *Life of Edwards*, p. 405. Hawley's letter is reprinted in *Jonathan Edwards: Representative Selections*, ed. Clarence H. Faust and Thomas H. Johnson, pp. 392–401. Edwards' remarks to his daughter appear in Samuel Hopkins, *Life and Character of Edwards*, p. 80.

on."[7] Although the family motif was in every way as vital to Edwards in his later work as it was in his earlier writings, we can seriously doubt that it much affected mid-eighteenth-century Puritan parishioners. Here, I think, lies an important element in the tragedy of his career. Whereas for Edwards this image, revelatory of a fundamental design of Providence, was still vibrant with meaning and emotion, for his parishioners it remained merely a part of a dead rhetorical convention stripped of the emotional overtones it once conveyed to earlier Puritans.

II. *The Telescopic Inner Eye*

The seventeen-year-old mission at Stockbridge was located at the edge of the wilderness. Although it did not completely insulate Edwards from repercussions arising from the Northampton episode, this isolated setting must to some extent have suited him. He had always been retiring and contemplative. It was here, despite attention to pastoral duties and practical affairs, that he investigated more deeply the inner regions of the self, especially its chief faculty. The will or heart always figured centrally in his thinking as the power most vitally involved in the drama of conversion. In 1754, "after many hindrances, delays, and interruptions," he published *A Careful and Strict Enquiry into the Modern Prevailing Notions of That Freedom of the Will, Which Is Supposed to Be Essential to Moral Agency, Virtue and Vice, Reward and Punishment, Praise and Blame*.[8]

This book reiterates a traditional doctrine which had become increasingly unpopular in eighteenth-century America. It is true that during the Great Awakening the New Lights had taught dogma stressing man's helpless dependence upon God, but it is also true that to some extent their practice undermined their doctrines.

[7] *Works* (Austin), 3:409. Sacvan Bercovitch interestingly observes that "the sharpening alienation of the ministers . . . emerges through the very vehemency of their commitment; the more tenaciously they uphold the ideal, the more they seem to be talking to themselves (and for themselves)" ("Horologicals to Chronometricals: The Puritan Jeremiad," p. 71).

[8] The quotation is from a letter Edwards wrote on April 14, 1753, printed in Dwight, *Life of Edwards*, p. 533. The edition used for Edwards' treatise on the will is *Freedom of the Will*, ed. Paul Ramsey.

Their Presbyterian tendency to regard large numbers of men as visible saints and their focus on the authority of each individual saint concerning his own spiritual condition tended to counter the Calvinist notion of the human will presented in New Light sermons. The Old Lights too, as we have already noted, contributed to the disintegration of the older Puritan idea of the will by attributing rational abilities to man which considerably reduced his sense of helplessness. Both forces, then, each in their own way, contributed to the political and economic factors influencing the greater sense of independence felt by the New Englanders of 1750, little more than two decades before the Revolutionary War.

This is the setting for Edwards' book. In his eyes the issue was simple: if the human will were really self-determining, if it were really free of predetermining causes, then no moral datum or absolute existed by means of which one could evaluate human actions in terms of reward and punishment, and God would be reduced to a mere caretaker of a world in which He continually discovers what men do ex post facto. For Edwards, on the contrary, God's absolute sovereignty is the necessary a priori factor at the center of any action or fact and, therefore, at the heart of self-definition.

Edwards defines the will as "that faculty or power or principle of mind by which it is capable of choosing." By *choice* he means such acts of volition as "approving, disapproving, liking, disliking, embracing, rejecting, determining, directing, commanding, forbidding, inclining or being averse, a being pleased or displeased with." But, he asks, are those modes of choice free or determined? In his view the fact that every choice results from one's strongest motive argues that the will is not free; motives, albeit frequently hidden from the conscious mind, actually determine inclination and choice. Edwards' introspection had led him to the psychological verity that our thoughts, words, and deeds are often expressions of unconscious motivations.

In his attempt to define human responsibility in *Freedom of the Will*, Edwards probed still more deeply into the nature of man's inner self. Significantly, he observes in his prefatory remarks that "of all kinds of knowledge that we can ever obtain, the knowledge of God, and the knowledge of ourselves, are the most important." Both are mutually related, and it is noteworthy that the world of nature or reference to the external world is not included specifically in this comment. Edwards, of course, never repudiated the reality of nature or its typical revelation of divine Will, but he had steadily moved toward the conclusion that knowledge of God is better revealed within the narrow circle of the private, insular self than in the expanses of the universe. Knowledge of the self is achieved by means of "right apprehensions concerning those two chief faculties of our nature, the *understanding* and *will*." These two powers, really inseparable, together comprise the cornerstone of the entire self. Echoing the older idea of an inner hierarchy within the soul, Edwards explains that "in some sense, the will always follows the last dictate of the understanding" and together they regulate the body: "The motions or state of the body are matter of command, only as they are subject to the soul, and connected with its acts." Thus, by the term *self* Edwards means the whole man (soul and body engaged in thought, word, and deed), which is nevertheless best scrutinized in terms of its *most* central component: "the soul has no other faculty whereby it can, in the most direct and proper sense, consent, yield to, or comply with any command, but the faculty of the will." As a synecdoche for the whole man, the will provides the best index to one's self. In fact, a man is his will.

Since reason and will constitute the natural image of God, introspection or self-knowledge is related to man's apprehension of his Creator. Here, as we have seen elsewhere, lies a key to Edwards' portrait of the inner self as a luminary, the light of which reveals something of the divine reality. In *Religious Affections* he used this image in order to describe the elect, observing that "the light of the Sun of Righteousness don't only shine upon them, but is so communicated to them that they shine also, and become little images of that Sun which shines upon them." This inner light discloses something about its source. Appropriately, Edwards alludes to this image in *Freedom of the Will* when contending that sin is not the product of an actual volition on God's part. To believe this, he suggests, is "as strange as it would be to argue, because it is always dark when the sun is gone, and never dark when the sun is present, that therefore all darkness is from the sun, and that his disk and beams must needs be black." As he indicated in *Religious*

Affections, the trouble with the sinful heart is that it is not a "light-some body" or luminary.

Such imagery is not accidental. Edwards was very much interested in the nature of language, as the "Personal Narrative" intimated. From Locke he had learned that words originate from the sensorium, although they rarely are as clear as the senses tend to be and may be employed to signify actions or motions quite removed from the senses. The defectiveness of language, Edwards believed, stems from its very dependence on the external world. Language is particularly "very deficient, in regard of terms to express precise truth concerning our own minds, and their faculties and operations."[9] At the core of this limitation is the fact that "words were first formed to express external things; and those that are applied to express things internal and spiritual, are almost all borrowed, and used in a sort of figurative sense." The Puritan mind and Locke had always been cautious about the dangers of figurative language, and properly speaking Edwards was never addicted to lavish displays of figurative language, even in his earlier writings. Edwards' introspection, his penetration of the inner self, steadily reduced the place of nature in his thinking; one might rightly surmise that imagery derived from nature became less serviceable to him in his exploration of the self as it became less meaningful to him as a source of divine revelation. Edwards was discovering that the internal landscape of the self (inclination) is for man more revelatory of divine reality than the external world (intention). From this perspective we can better understand Edwards' concern over the limits of language, especially his anti-Lockean distrust of its dependence on the external world.

His struggle in *Freedom of the Will* to make language and the natural world convey some sense of man's inner being may be illustrated by a lengthy passage in which he tries to explain how, from God's perspective, each future action of any will appears "as if it had already been; inasmuch as *in effect* it actually exists already." In order to depict this relation, he refers to the images of

9 For good discussions of Locke's influence on Edwards' view of language, see Perry Miller's "The Rhetoric of Sensation," in his *Errand into the Wilderness*, pp. 167–183, and Edward H. Davidson, "From Locke to Edwards," *Journal of the History of Ideas* 24 (July 1963): 355–372.

heavenly bodies reflected in a telescope. These images, he indicates, "have had a past actual existence, and it is become utterly impossible now that it should be otherwise than that they have existed." He then asks the reader to "suppose future existences some way or other to have influence back, to produce effects beforehand, and cause exact and perfect images of themselves in a glass, a thousand years before they exist." These images, he continues, "are real effects of these future existences, perfectly dependent on, and connected with their cause; these effects and images, having already had actual existence, rendering that matter of their existing perfectly firm and stable, and utterly impossible to be otherwise; this proves in like manner as in the other instance, that the existence of the things which are their causes is also equally sure, firm, and necessary; and that it is alike impossible but that they should be, as if they had been already, as their effects have." Although the immediate focus of this argument is nature, we should not lose sight of the fact that it is the analogy that Edwards stresses. The images in the passage are internalized in the sense that the thrust of Edwards' comment is finally not outward into the heavens but inward upon the luminary of the self. "Instead of images in a glass," we are supposed to imagine "the antecedent effects to be perfect ideas of them in the divine mind"; this is the crucial step in the analogy. Since the divine Mind and the human mind are related—that is, since the elect reflect both a natural image of their Creator and something of His excellency—whenever the saint turns his telescopic eye within, he gazes upon a moonlike self mirroring divine reality.

As in his earlier work, Edwards' exploration of the self is supported by his doctrinal alignment with the collective self of Puritan orthodoxy. We should bear in mind, then, that *Freedom of the Will* defends a conservative position in Puritan thought and was quite out of touch with the times. A significant indication of Edwards' traditionality appears in his final remarks in the work. Here he scolds his opponents, urging them to consider "whether many of the first Reformers, and others that succeeded them, whom God in their day made the chief pillars of his church, and greatest instruments of their deliverance from error and darkness, and of the support of the cause of piety among them, have not been injured, in the contempt with which they have been treated by many late writers." Reiterating a specific complaint he made in *An Humble Attempt*, this comment is simultaneously a plea for respect for orthodoxy (as Edwards interpreted it) and a prophecy of the doom which threatened New England as a consequence of subverting the hierarchy represented by this tradition. The latter element emerges still more clearly in Edwards' contention that Arminians "despise" and challenge "their fathers with such magisterial assurance." For Edwards, as we have seen throughout his work, the father image is important because it implies hierarchical order as well as traditional continuity. By mentioning this image, even so briefly, he reminds the dissenters of their heritage and of their proper position in the divine scheme. Man "is capable of falling in with God's ends, and what he sees his Creator aim at, and co-operating with him," Edwards remarks elsewhere, "or of setting himself against the Creator's designs. It is manifest, that it is the Creator's design, that parents should nourish their children, and that children should be subject to their parents."[10]

This passage pinpoints exactly the implication behind Edwards' indictment of his opponents in the final pages of *Freedom of the Will*; they are rebellious children whose heretical theology indicates their spiritual malaise. Disregarding finesse and wielding the weight of tradition, he completes his indictment by intentionally structuring the last section of the treatise in such a way that it explicitly affirms the articles of faith established by the Synod of Dort. In 1619 this Synod condemned the Arminians and reasserted the five chief principles of Calvinism: total depravity, unconditional election, limited atonement, irresistible grace, and the perseverance of the saints. *Freedom of the Will* concludes with an emphasis on these same five tenets. For Edwards the divine truth revealed at the core of such orthodox Puritan dogma is identical to that reflected by the inner self illuminated by special grace.

III. *The Disposition of the Heart*

By May, 1757, Edwards had completed another treatise designed to buttress several of the arguments presented in *Freedom of*

10 *Works* (Austin), 7:365.

the Will as well as to confront emerging popular notions regarding man's innate nature, especially as set forth in John Taylor's *The Scripture-Doctrine of Original Sin, Proposed to Free and Candid Examination.* The new work, entitled *The Great Christian Doctrine of Original Sin Defended,* was already in press when Edwards died in 1758. It was published posthumously the same year. Apparently he had originally planned to include this treatise as part of a larger work which would contain, as well, sections on true virtue and God's purpose in creating the world.

Although not as smoothly argued as *Freedom of the Will, Original Sin* is a remarkably clear and well-reasoned document. It defends a basic tenet of Puritanism, namely that all men are depraved, that "the heart of man is naturally of a corrupt and evil disposition."[11] By 1757 this was a considerably less acceptable notion than it had been previously. Too much intellectual and economic change had occurred in America to permit the implications of this Calvinistic doctrine to continue to thrive. Many thinkers of the time not only saw the earth as part of a rationally designed universe of plentitude and possibility, but they also believed man to be endowed with a self, with reason and will, enabling him to realize the potentialities of his inner nature in relation to the outer world. According to some eighteenth-century spokesmen, man possessed an innately benevolent disposition; though prone to err in his presently uncultivated circumstances, he was theoretically capable of actually improving himself and the entire human race.

Edwards disagreed. Defending the traditional Puritan view of man, he contended that all humanity shares in Adam's fall from grace, with the result that all men are born "with a tendency to sin, and to misery and ruin for their sin, which actually will be the consequence, unless mere grace steps in and prevents it." To substantiate this doctrine he observed that, despite mankind's wide distribution on the face of the earth, people everywhere have revealed a proneness to sin. Edwards intended this point to counter an eighteenth-century belief that men become evil only because they have been adversely influenced by detrimental environments. In point of fact, Edwards contended, even after considering all the

[11] Quotations are from *Original Sin,* ed. Clyde A. Holbrook.

various environments in the world, nowhere is there a person exempt from wickedness. It follows, he concluded, that since the world is not evil itself—no eighteenth-century thinker could say so and be consistent—then the defect must reside within man himself. He disallowed the claim that human disposition derives from "external circumstances" and argued that it "is inherent."

Edwards also refuted those of his contemporaries who claimed that the concept of innate depravity is repudiated by the example of people whose good actions exceed their bad ones. In Edwards' view, regardless how much alleged virtue a man manifests, merely a single trespass against God's perfect law, the least sin or moral imperfection, warrants his damnation. To prove this point Edwards makes effective use of the following illustration:

> It would be much more absurd, to suppose that such a state of nature is good, or not bad, under a notion of men's doing more honest and kind things, than evil ones; than to say, the state of that ship is good, to cross the Atlantick Ocean in, that is such as cannot hold together through the voyage, but will infallibly founder and sink by the way; under a notion that it may probably go great part of the way before it sinks, or that it will proceed and sail above water more hours than it will be sinking.

Edwards' image is drawn from the practical level of his reader's experience and couched in the empirical rhetoric appropriate to the times, but it also covertly includes a traditional dimension. In Puritan writings the image of a ship crossing an ocean represents a favorite analogy for the Christian pilgrim as a mariner sailing the seas of life toward the port of heaven. In early New England Puritan writings, this image is a cliché. Yet its traditional character permits Edwards to find in the empirical example a type for the spiritual truth concerning human depravity. He similarly succeeds in the following passage:

> how absurd must it be for Christians to object, against the depravity of man's nature, a greater number of innocent and kind actions, than of crimes; and to talk of a prevailing innocency, good nature, industry, and cheerfulness of the greater part of mankind? Infinitely more absurd, than it would be to insist, that the domestic of a prince was not a bad servant, because though sometimes he contemned and affronted his master to a great degree, yet he did not spit in his master's face so often as he performed acts

of service; or, than it would be to affirm, that his spouse was a good wife to him, because, although she committed adultery, and that with the slaves and scoundrals sometimes, yet she did not do this so often as she did the duties of a wife.

The logic and the instructive humor of these remarks are evident enough. These images possess, however, two levels of meaning in that beneath their experiential level lie the traditional Christian images of Christ as the Prince whom man is to serve and as the Bridegroom who marries the members of the church as His spouse. Infidelity in either relationship, whether in a secular or a spiritual sense, constitutes a serious infraction against the divine principle of hierarchical order which, in Edwards' view, pervades every aspect of existence. These images, reflecting Edwards' idea that the external world is a shadow of the internal one of the self, represent a neatly forged argument at once yoking empirical evidence and spiritual truth.

We might note in passing that Edwards' regard for hierarchical order, particularly as exemplified by the family unit, is also apparent in his remarks on posterity's share in the sin of Adam and Eve. Adam is the "moral," "common," "federal," and "public head and representative of his posterity." All men are members of the collective body of humanity governed by this head, or, to put the matter another way, Adam is our "first father" and we are his children. Because of our membership in his family, we inherit a proclivity to evil, a "depravity of nature, remaining an established principle in the heart of a child of Adam." Thus we are all culpable. Edwards' use of the family motif in this work is by no means as effective as it is in some of his earlier writings. In this instance it remains too thickly embedded in tradition and certainly could not have carried much weight for many of his contemporaries.

When he refutes the notions held by some of his contemporaries concerning the environmental origins of evil and when he qualifies the idea that mankind inherits guilt from its first father, Edwards focuses his attention, ultimately, on the inner self. *Original Sin* may at times rely on certain empirical observations, albeit frequently with a scriptural or theological dimension, but in fact it is little concerned with the external world. The human self is at its center, as it is in *Freedom of the Will.* "All moral qualities," Edwards explains at the very start of his book, "all principles, either of virtue or vice, lie in the disposition of the heart." What a man is depends on the inner landscape of his soul, the heart of which is an innately depraved, eclipsed luminary. It is the heart that must be fathomed if one is to discover his identity.

Identity or internal harmony, however, was lost when Adam willfully rebelled, asserting his natural principles (*flesh*) to an inordinate degree. The superior principles (*spirit*), which should "possess the throne, and maintain an absolute dominion in the heart," were forfeited as a result. Deprived of an inner sense of identity, the empty heart succumbs to delusions of self-grandeur. In the sinful state one's sense of self merely parodies true selfhood, for Adam's transgression "was a fatal catastrophe, a turning of all things upside down, and the succession of a state of the most odious and dreadful confusion." Bereft of the identity concommitant with this original inner order, fallen man cannot readily discern divine reality, which once was gloriously reflected by the inner self. For Edwards the real drama of Adam's fall from grace took place not in the garden of Eden but in the once paradisiacal terrain of his heart.

The centrality of the self in *Original Sin* is equally apparent in Edwards' discussion of the nature of evil. Predictably, he does not allow that sin has any foundation in relation to creation; that is, wickedness cannot be associated with existence or with the objective reality informing existence, because to do so would be to implicate God as the originator of evil. Though not wholly successful in exonerating God, Edwards makes clear, as he did in *Freedom of the Will,* that sin is not to be understood from a Manichean perspective. God *permits* sin by withholding the superior principles without which man remains defective spiritually. Sin arises from this deprivation. It does not, therefore, actually exist; it is a condition, a state of privation in the heart, the absence there of "the image and love of God." Sin, in other words, is from God's perspective only a mental defection from the divine Will, a rebellious disposition in the heart of the sinner. Since goodness, which pervades all of creation, supplies the only context in which sin occurs, then strictly speaking evil can have no mode of existence except in the mind of a person who dissents from this goodness. Sin, finally, is nothing else but a subjective, moral condition, and *innate depravity* is the term used to refer to the universal human tendency to yield to this perverse disposition of the will.

Sin's struggle for existence is doomed because the reality in which it must seek its being is divine Love. Man's will or self is inevitably defined in terms of this field of reality, for divine Love is the alpha and omega of everything. In the saint, as we have seen, the self brightens, so to speak, in proportion to its rediscovery and embracement of this reality. In the sinner, on the contrary, the self is eclipsed as a result of its rebellious and parodical relation to divine Love. Ironically, even the wicked heart, asserting self-love, must define itself with regard to that very divine reality against which it revolts. The heart of the unregenerate person possesses the same fundamental inclinations as are present in that of the saint, indeed in all of nature, but the sinner's will perverts these impulses: "evil affections radically consist in inordinate love to other things besides God." Sin is a perversion of love or a failure to love properly. Love constitutes the essence or definition of a genuine self. Self-love, when it serves as an end in itself, parodies true devotion, and this is why Edwards and other Puritans speak of conversion as "the turning of the heart."

Like *Freedom of the Will*, *Original Sin* attacks concepts of the self espoused by many of Edwards' contemporaries. In fact it subtly implies that dissenters from the doctrine of original sin are in effect bearing witness to its truth, for in their position they give vent to "a foolish self-exaltation and pride," whereas acknowledgement of the doctrine "tends to promote humility." Edwards tenaciously held to tradition. His meditative inquiries into the regions of the self, now reinforced by his physical isolation at Stockbridge, lay at the core of his defense of this increasingly unpopular doctrine. Convinced of the truth confirmed by his exploration of the luminary self, he asserted with assurance, in the concluding paragraph of the book, that his opponents' imperfect views resulted from "looking through a cloudy and delusory medium." What he had discerned at the core of the self and of Puritan orthodoxy had become the polestar guiding him through the metaphysical wilderness of the eastern frontier of his exile at Stockbridge.

IV. *Of Beauty and Virtue*

For seven years Edwards served at Stockbridge. Whenever he could at Northampton, he had generally enjoyed spending up to fourteen hours a day in his study, so he must have found the relative isolation of the mission pleasing to some degree once he overcame his initial discomfort. It was while he was stationed here (in 1757) that he received an invitation to become president of the College of New Jersey, later named Princeton College. The trustees of the school had had him in mind for the post for some time. His visits during many of the commencements provided opportunities for them to refresh their interest in him. They must no doubt have dismissed Edwards' conservative position on church membership as of little consequence to the post of presidency; perhaps they better understood his intentions, penetrating the bad publicity and downright chicanery surrounding his dismissal from Northampton. They certainly must have appreciated his intellectual reputation and such views on the need for an educated clergy as he had expressed in, say, *Some Thoughts*.

In reply to this invitation, Edwards listed finances, poor health, and several personal shortcomings which, in his opinion, disqualified him as a likely candidate for the position. Of primary importance, we might surmise, was his concern over the writing he had planned to do. In the letter he sent the board, he noted that study and writing "have long engaged and swallowed up my mind, and been the chief entertainment and delight of my life."[12] He unconsciously revealed both the public and the private aspects of his work; it has been "for benefitting my fellow creatures" and "for my own benefit" that he has devoted so much energy to his writings. What he has written represents—to use his own metaphor—a kind of travelling, and, he noted, "the farther I travelled in this way, the more and wider the field opened." The field steadily unveiled to him was not only theology but the self which he had explored in the context of the traditions of his religion.

[12] This letter is printed in Dwight, *Life of Edwards*, pp. 568–571.

When he explained, "My heart is so much in these studies," he was indicating the degree to which the inner domain had become for him a revelation of divine reality. He frankly preferred introspection to external prestige.

That he was finally prevailed upon to abandon his privacy at Stockbridge does not suggest a change of heart. This decision, on the contrary, attests to Edwards' complete willingness to comply with and trust in what he discerned to be God's Will in the matter. If God meant that he should take this position, if it were intended as a further development of the pattern designed for his life, so be it. As we have seen, Edwards was particularly vigilant in looking for underlying designs; perhaps his rise and fall in Northampton was now to be followed by another ascent for God's cause. His final decision to go to New Jersey, of course, did not negate the sacrifice involved in his forsaking, at the age of fifty-four, the private life he loved so well. Within a month of his arrival at the college he lay dying, infected from a smallpox inoculation. The pattern was now complete: a second rise followed by still another descent, one last rapid test of the self's love and humility.

After his death two works, "The Nature of True Virtue" and "Dissertation Concerning the End for Which God Created the World," were published as *Two Dissertations* (1765). Written while Edwards was at Stockbridge and originally intended as part of one treatise which was to include his study of original sin, both works document his introspective frame of mind.

In "The Nature of True Virtue" Edwards defends intuition as a way of knowing, superior to information gathered by means of the senses. This position involves, of course, a further development of the arguments advanced in *A Divine and Supernatural Light* and in *Religious Affections*. Even in *A Faithful Narrative* he had described how the saint intuitively feels the evidence of the spirit dwelling within him. Edwards' emphasis on intuition in "The Nature of True Virtue" is indicative of his view of the inner self as a more vital source of revelation than the external world.

His argument is to a significant extent based on his definition of two sorts of beauty. There is *particular beauty*, by which he means anything appearing beautiful when it is viewed within the limited purview of the perceiver. *General beauty*, on the other hand, refers to something that is beautiful "when viewed most perfectly, comprehensively and universally."[13] For Edwards virtue must be defined with regard to these two terms. Virtue is the "beauty belonging to Beings that have perception and will"; its "original seat" is "in the mind." True virtue is related to general beauty, not particular beauty. It consists in genuine love for and benevolence to being-in-general (God).

To be truly virtuous the self must be purged of any taint of pride, and its identity must necessarily derive from a complete alignment with the divine Self or being-in-general. No son of Adam, while living on earth, is capable of true virtue. Fallen men are prone to rebellion, and "beauty does not consist in discord and dissent, but in consent and agreement." Deluded by its subjective experience of seeming independence, the corrupt heart cannot express the love of God requisite for this alignment. The unregenerate self lacks "that consent, propensity and union of heart to Being in general" because "all sin has its source from selfishness, or from selflove not subordinate to regard for Being in general." That selflove does not in itself constitute an evil, Edwards argued elsewhere. Only when it perversely serves as one's *raison d'être*, only when it is not circumscribed by love of God, does it lead to sin: "though selflove is far from being useless in the world, yea, it is exceeding necessary to society, yet every body sees that if it be not subordinate to, and regulated by, another more extensive principle, it may make a man a common enemy to the system he is related to." Among other things, this statement summarizes the implications of the father motif occurring throughout Edwards' work as well as underscores his affinity to the collective self he discerned at the heart of Puritan tradition.

The preceding comments indicate that "The Nature of True Virtue" is less concerned with the specific deeds of men in the world than with the source of these actions in the heart. Virtue should not, in Edwards' view, be judged in relation to one's external deeds. Virtue "is the beauty of those qualities and acts of the mind, that are of a moral nature." Above all else the will is particularly involved. In fact, virtue cannot be said to belong "merely to speculation; but to the disposition of the will, or . . . the

[13] "The Nature of True Virtue," in *Works* (Austin), 2:393–471.

heart." The presence or absence of virtue, therefore, is determined by whether or not the love of the self is genuine and arises from an identification with God.

In his discussion of beauty and virtue, Edwards reveals further his predilection for the inner self over nature as a revelation of divine reality. As the Second Book, nature is undeniably beautiful. Even inanimate nature demonstrates "a mutual consent and agreement of different things in form, manner, quantity, and visible end or design." Such characteristics as "regularity, order, uniformity, symmetry, proportion, harmony" comprise the beauty of nature. All of these attributes, however, represent only particular beauty, an "inferior, secondary beauty." "Material things can have analogy to things spiritual," Edwards explains, but "they can have no more than a shadow" or image of being's consent to Being or of "the union of minds or spiritual Beings in a mutual propensity and affection of heart." Thus, in his opinion, nature manifests a "natural union or agreement" rather than a "cordial agreement," which consists "in concord and union of mind and heart." (This distinction between natural and cordial agreement is doubtless related to the difference between common and special grace remarked in our discussion of *A Divine and Supernatural Light*.) The role of nature is, finally, "to assist those whose hearts are under the influence of a truly virtuous temper."

Since the natural world is merely an image, albeit an excellent one, of the beauty between minds in agreement, then it must provide a less immediate and lucid revelation of the divine reality than the heart of the saint (conversely, it provides a better source of revelation than the heart of the sinner, whom nature indicts). Men are "stupified by sensual objects and appetites" not because the latter are inherently detrimental but because they concern particulars. The mind can exist in a more direct relation to the totality of divine reality. The saint in fact comes to know God principally on account of his exploration of the inner self. "We never could have any notion what understanding or volition, love or hatred are, either in created spirits or in God," Edwards writes, "if we had never experienced what understanding and volition, love and hatred, are in our own minds. Knowing what they are by consciousness, we can add degrees, and deny limits, and remove changeableness and other imperfections, and ascribe them to God." Reason, will, and affections (soul and body)—these constitute the gamut of one's self. It follows, then, that the exploration of the heart, in the light of Scripture, provides the saint with the best intimation of divine reality. What the saint discovers within is an intuitive knowledge, a reflection of general beauty not dependent on the senses of the body and on the external world.

Edwards once again resorts to the honey image he had used in the past in order to make his discussion clearer. No argumentation can convey to anyone the sweet taste of honey. One simply must experience it for himself. Likewise, he contends, the "manner of being affected with the immediate presence of the beautiful idea depends not, therefore, on any reasonings about the idea, after we have it"; in actuality it relies "on the frame of our minds, whereby they are so made that such an idea, as soon as we have it, is grateful, or appears beautiful." Edwards internalizes the senses, so to speak; the heart perceives or tastes by means of an inward sensation, which is to say by intuition: "the way we come by the idea or sensation of beauty, is by immediate sensation of the gratefulness of the idea called beautiful." When it indeed loves being-in-general, the mind of the saint becomes enlarged, as it were, and is inclined "to feel, to desire, and to act" as if it were one with God. In the saint the divine image, spiritual (intuitive) and natural (rational), is partially renewed, with the result that his self is more attuned to God's Will and becomes a luminary mirroring the light emanating from the divine Self.

V. *Eternally Tending*

The "Dissertation Concerning the End for Which God Created the World" is in several respects reminiscent of *God Glorified*. In the earlier work, it may be recalled, the central idea that "all that we have is of God, and through him, and in him" nearly becomes a refrain. The "Dissertation" similarly stresses that "the whole is of God, and in God, and to God."[14] Basic to both of these works is the tenet of God's absolute sovereignty and man's total dependence. Beyond this point of similarity, however, such a comparison be-

[14] Quotations are from *Works* (Austin), 6:9–124.

comes deceptive. There is a distinct qualitative difference between the two works. In the rigid prose of *God Glorified*, Edwards emphasizes the distance between man and God, the gap between human dereliction and divine sublimity. During the years of his ministry, this sense of distance narrowed in his writings, as we have seen. God is utterly superior to His creation in every regard, but He is not as remote as man tends to think. Actually the abyss man perceives between himself and God is an illusion, an internal sensation resulting from the blinding subjective disposition of his rebellious will. For the saint, as "The Nature of True Virtue" indicates, there is indeed no such separation, rather a heartfelt union and agreement with the Creator. The "Dissertation" celebrates the intimate, mystical relation between God and the regenerate will.

When He creates and as He renews that creation at every moment, God communicates "benevolence or love." This means, without contradicting the idea of an *ex nihilo* creation, that God communicates something of His very essence. Nevertheless, creation itself does not provide, in Edwards' view, a sufficiently worthy end for this expression, which means that the divine communication must actually be circular with God Himself as the ultimate goal. Yet, since everything in existence is included in this circle at some point, a real bond exists between creation and Creator: "God and the creature, in this affair of emanation of the divine fulness, are not properly set in opposition"; "God's respect to the creature's good, and his respect to himself, is not a divided respect; but both are united in one, as the happiness of the creature aimed at, is happiness in union with itself." In the "Dissertation" Edwards gives full expression to the tendency in his writings, subsequent to *God Glorified*, to bridge the gulf between man and God. In the "Dissertation" he explains that man is "infinitely, nearly, and closely united to God."

The sinful heart is perverse in that it futilely rebels against the very context of its being and identity, parodying the reality it cannot in point of fact escape. True selfhood, as the saint discovers, is defined entirely, inevitably, in terms of the circularity of God's communication. In order to participate in this ultimate circle, however, the saint must first penetrate the onion-like layers of self-love. This means, in one sense, that in its quest for true identity the saint's heart must, in striving for alignment with the circularity of God's communication, always seek larger circles of definition beyond the restricting borders of self-love. The collective self at the core of Puritan tradition represents one such expanded context which appealed to Edwards, one particularly associated with the father motif so prevalent in his writings. Even in the "Dissertation" a vestige of this motif survives. In one passage he remarks that true identity emerges only when "the interest of the creature, is, as it were, God's own interest, in proportion to the degree of their relation and union to God. Thus the interest of a man's family is looked upon as the same with his own interest; because of the relation they stand in to him; his propriety in them, and their strict union with him." Again he reminds his readers, "if by reason of the strictness of the union of a man and his family, their interest may be looked upon as one, how much more one is the interest of Christ and his church, (whose first union in heaven is unspeakably more perfect and exalted than that of an earthly father and his family)."

For Edwards the image of the family nearly always implied the larger context crucial to the self's attainment of identity. In the "Dissertation" this motif is poorly developed because Edwards was writing of the ultimate circle circumscribing all of creation; in creating, God is His own end: "He had regard to it, as an emanation from himself, and a communication of himself, and as the thing communicated, in its nature returned to himself, as its final term." At one level Edwards was countering a trend in eighteenth-century thought designating man as the final end of God's act of creation. For Edwards such a notion was blatantly absurd. At a more personal level he was extending truths he had derived from his discovery that the heart was a key to divine reality. In effect he defined the entire universe in terms of his insight into the saint's luminary self.

We have noted throughout Edwards' work the centrality of the image of reflected sunlight. In *Original Sin* it served as a means of explaining God's continuous reassertion or re-creation of all existence *ex nihilo*. After indicating that "God's preserving created things in being is perfectly equivalent to a continued creation, or to his creating those things out of nothing at each moment of their existence," he refers to the moon as an analogy or type of this truth because its reflected brightness appears constant, although in actuality "it ceases, and is renewed, in each successive point of time; and so becomes altogether a new effect at each instant." What we see is similar to a reflection in a mirror, where the object and the image appear "precisely the same, with a continuing perfect identity." The fact remains, however, that "all dependent existence whatsoever is in a constant flux."

In the "Dissertation" Edwards writes, "Light is the external expression, exhibition and manifestation of the excellency of the luminary, of the sun for instance." Whatever is illuminated derives its identity from the source of the light it reflects: "it is by a participation of this communication from the sun, that surrounding objects receive all their lustre, beauty and brightness." God, for whom the sun is a type, is the ultimate source of this illumination or identity, both in nature and in the moonlike self. God is "an infinite fountain of light" shining "forth in beams of communicated knowledge and understanding." Since God serves as His own end, the light or being He emanates reflects back to Him; his fulness is received and returned. Here is both emanation and remanation," Edwards explains, adding that "the refulgence shines upon and into the creature, and is reflected back to the luminary. The beams of glory come from God, and are something of God, and are refunded back again to their original. So that the whole is of God, and in God, and to God, and God is the beginning, middle and end in this affair." If it is not eclipsed by sin, then, the self is included in this circuit of divine self-communication.

For Edwards conversion is in fact typified by the progression of the lunar phases from new to full moon. "The moon as it comes nearer the sun," Edwards recorded in his notebook, "grows darker and darker; so the soul, the more it is fitted for Christ, is more and more emptied of itself that it may be filled with Christ."[15] The true meaning or identity of the self derives from the divine illumination it reflects back to its source, for just as God "delights in his own light, he must delight in every beam of that light." Edwards likens the soul not only to the moon but to a jewel which derives its luster and its value from the way in which it reflects light.

[15] *Images or Shadows of Divine Things*, p. 72.

The inner self of the saint best reflects this communication because its principal components (the understanding and will, man's natural image of God) are related to the divine fullness, the source of God's communication and glory: "the fulness of the God-head is the fulness of his understanding, consisting in his knowledge, and the fulness of his will, consisting in his virtue and happiness. And therefore the external glory of God consists in the communication of these." The saint's inner self is equipped to receive this communication. In an essay on the Trinity, Edwards wrote that "our souls are made in the Image of God, we have understanding & will, Idea & Love as God hath, and the difference is only in the Perfection of degree and manner."[16] Thus, as the "Dissertation" argues, since it is "created in the image of God; even as having these two faculties of understanding and will," the inner self becomes the primary locus of divine expression: "God communicates himself to the understanding of the creature, in giving him the knowledge of his glory; and to the will of the creature, in giving him holiness, consisting primarily in the love of God." Though all of creation reflects the divine light or emanation, man's inner self, when gracious, provides the fullest reflection of divine reality.

Although the reception of this light or grace in the soul is immediate, its influence, as *A Faithful Narrative* and *A History of the Work of Redemption* indicate, is progressive for the saint experiencing degrees of improvement. Just as the unfolding of history provides an allegory of the soul's progress toward God, so also do the movements of nature. In God's grand design all of creation exists in a "constant and eternal motion," forever returning to its Creator. Everything steadily advances "nearer and nearer to him through all eternity." The closer everything in creation approaches God, the more it fulfills itself. Of course, created matter never merges with its source; it eternally tends.

This very principle of upward ascendancy provides the motive energy behind the saint's effort to abandon the narrow confines of self-love and to seek identity in relation to the more pervasive context of divine fullness, glory, and love. To God "belongs all the heart." As the saint's self is progressively aligned with the divine Will, as his heart finds itself "more and more conformed to God,"

[16] *An Unpublished Essay of Edwards on the Trinity*, p. 77.

it becomes steadily attuned to the underlying principle of creation: "the eternally increasing union of the saints with God, by something that is ascending constantly towards that infinite height, moving upwards with a given velocity, and that is to continue thus to move to all eternity." To be in accord with this motion—that is the answer to Edwards' search for identity. "The creature is no further happy," he explains, "than he becomes one with God," and this condition depends on the progressive workings of grace, for "the more those divine communications increase in the creature, the more it becomes one with God." With the light of special grace the self becomes a true luminary mirroring the divine reality informing everything. True identity arises from an internal paradise regained, from the increasing restoration of the image of God in the soul: "the image is more and more perfect, and so the good that is in the creature comes nearer and nearer to an identity with that which is in God."

The "Dissertation" succeeds in bridging the gap between man and God. In personal terms the work may have struck Edwards as very special indeed. Behind his hesitation to accept the position at the College of New Jersey may well have been a sensitivity to the implications of his Stockbridge writings. Surely he could not have been unaware of the lucidity and the sureness of his treatment of complex issues in his last works. Was this not a sign from God, another clue to the minister's own spiritual condition, a further unfolding of his personal narrative? Did not divine light and inspiration shine forth through these writings? Indeed, just as creation is the "emanation and true external expression of God's internal glory and fulness"—by internal glory is meant God's Understanding and Will—so too Edwards' manuscripts represent external expressions of his verbal inner self; and if these works reveal the light of divine truth, then surely that light is likewise to be found in his inner self (understanding and will), the source of these writings. Surely, too, by now his exile at Stockbridge would have seemed less a divine indictment than the fulfillment of a hope he had expressed in a letter to Thomas Gillespie (July 1, 1751), that his experience at the mission would "improve me as an instrument of his glory, and the good of the souls of mankind."[17]

[17] Dwight, *Life of Edwards*, p. 465.

His writings were an expression of the whole self, consisting of "knowing, esteeming, loving, rejoicing in, and praising God." The self should not remain merely passive, merely the recipient of light, but must actively participate in it through the use of the understanding and will: "A main difference between the intelligent and moral parts, and the rest of the world, lies in this, that the former are capable of knowing their creator, and the end for which he made them, and capable of actively complying with his design in their creation and promoting it; while other creatures cannot promote the design of their creation, only passively and eventually." In the "Dissertation" Edwards actively completes the circle wherein God first communicates externally His "internal glory to created understandings" and then, in turn, the recipient expresses himself, relating his "high esteem of God, love to God, and complacence and joy in God." Through his works Edwards contributes to mankind's upward ascent toward the Creator. In completing the circle he asserts his selfhood, a sense of selfhood now truly defined with regard to the reality of the divine Self. Devout expression— mental (thought), spoken (word), written (deed) in response to the divine communication evident in Scripture, the self, history, and nature—constitutes the true end of the regenerate self. Such devotion becomes the self's highest end, the only appropriate response to the "immediate communication between the Creator and [man,] this highest of creatures according to the order of being,"[18] just as "that nature in a tree, by which it puts forth buds, shoots out branches, and brings forth leaves and fruits, is a disposition that terminates in its own complete self." When it is aligned to the divine Will, when it actively participates in the ascent of all creation, the self possesses identity; in fact it then *is* indeed a self.

Whereas *Freedom of the Will* and *Original Sin* may be read as efforts to reduce man's illusion of free will and self-sufficiency, the "Dissertation" celebrates the discovery of genuine selfhood. God, to be sure, remains the alpha and omega of existence, the ultimate cause and effect. He "is the first author of their being and motion, so he is the last end." But the individual self of the saint does not suffocate within this boundary. Rather, it thrives because

[18] *The Philosophy of Jonathan Edwards*, p. 127.

this larger dimension of expanded familial rings of meaning frees the self from the imprisoning constriction of subjective delusion. It is, as "The Justice of God in the Damnation of Sinners" makes clear, the wicked who are choked within the ring of perverse selfhood and who, paradoxically, find themselves outside the circle of God's city. Equally paradoxical is the fact that as his context of selfhood expands, the saint discerns God to be not only the outermost circle but also the inmost center of everything, especially of the self. Thus the saint is freed from himself—and this signifies an important distinction between Edwards' notion of the self and that of the antinomians—in order that he may discover who he truly is.

Regarding the style of this much undervalued work, we should not ignore Edwards' complaint, once again, about the limits of language resulting from its bondage to the external world: "I confess there is a degree of indistinctness and obscurity in the close consideration of such subjects, and a great imperfection in the expressions we use concerning them, arising unavoidably from the infinite sublimity of the subject, and the incomprehensibleness of those things that are divine." These comments suggest why so few images surface in the "Dissertation," why the language tends toward abstraction. External nature and the inner self may be radically related, but finally the inner realm is of a higher order of divine revelation, into which language can provide only a glimpse. Nevertheless, the language of the "Dissertation" does succeed in conveying Edwards' inward vision. The sheer effusiveness and fluidity of its cumulative sentences stand in marked contrast to the conscious parallelism and periodic sentences of many of his early sermons, particularly *God Glorified*. An assurance of tone is evident in this work, not an unwavering certitude in his election but rather a personal fortitude and identity arising from a felt sense of the mystical relation between the inner self and God.

[6]

Pastor and Prophet: Conclusion

As one might expect, contemporary assessments of Edwards' work were mixed. Ezra Stiles speculated in his diary that within a generation Edwards' writings would "pass into as transient Notice perhaps scarce above Oblivion, as Willard or Twiss, or Norton; and when Posterity occasionally comes across them in the Rubbish of Libraries, the rare Characters who may read & be pleased with them, will be looked upon as singular & whimsical."[1] Gilbert Tennant, on the other hand, spoke of him as an "ascending Elijah."[2] Later Samuel Hopkins would write: "President Edwards, in the esteem of all the judicious, who were well acquainted with him, either personally, or by his writings, was one of the greatest—best —and most useful of men, that have lived in this age."[3] More recent assessments have been somewhat more uniform, generally viewing Edwards as one of the most brilliant defenders of Puritanism.

With regard to Edwards' appraisal of his own life and work, it is difficult to know for certain what he felt. The Northampton failure weighed heavily upon his mind; yet the success of his writings must have seemed a sign of divine favor. Ultimately, as the "Personal Narrative" indicates, the question of success or failure was meaningless when asked within a temporal frame of reference. One's outward circumstances, though they indeed mean something, are frequently bewildering to the person involved in them. Even

[1] *The Literary Diary of Ezra Stiles*, ed. Franklin Bowditch Dexter, 3:275.
[2] See David Bostwick, *Self Disclaimed, and Christ Exalted*, pp. 31–32.
[3] Samuel Hopkins, *Life and Character of Edwards*, p. 1.

the very terms *success* and *failure* prove delusive, as does the simple dichotomy they imply. God's ways are mysterious, beyond human ken. They are, nonetheless, consistent and progressive. What mattered to Edwards was less his external condition than the solution to his internal unrest. True success or failure for a Puritan was finally defined in terms of his spiritual development. Edwards could be certain that he had experienced an inward growth, a steady development that kept him active in the service of Christ even, and especially, during the seemingly ignominious exile at Stockbridge.

In his quest for inner identity he aligned himself with Puritan orthodoxy. His moderate position in the controversies between the Old and the New Lights arose from an effort to make new ideas conform to established Puritan dogma. In Puritan tradition, that most significant revelation of the underlying continuity of all history, Edwards discerned a collective self, an inner identity manifesting the intent of the divine Will. The recognition of this source of meaning informed his narrow, tenacious interpretation of the term *visible saints*, the Lord's Supper, original sin, and predestination. He was no precursor of modern thought. At best Edwards was a moderate with a distinct prejudice, which deepened over the years, for the traditions of the Puritan past. For him real departures from established conventions, as distinct from merely further clarifications of them, signified the failure of the New Israelites.

At the center of Edwards' traditionalism was a respect for order. In his view the numerous movements of nature, the successive events of history, and the progressive experiences of the gracious soul all derived from and tended toward God. Order characterized the emanation of divine beauty.[4] It was with this in mind that Edwards spoke of the "beauty or order in society" in "The Nature of True Virtue." In a genuine society, he argued, members "have all their appointed office, place and station, according to their several capacities and talents, and every one keeps his place, and continues in his proper business." This remark implies a point of view increasingly unacceptable to Americans in the years preceding the

---

[4] See Roland A. Delattre, *Beauty and Sensibility in the Thought of Jonathan Edwards*, pp. 111–114. Even heaven is chiefly characterized by its social order (*Works* [Dwight], 8:489).

Revolutionary War. For Edwards, however, the comment had less
to do with politics than with defending an idea fundamental to his
inherited myth of social order in early New England.

His concern with order, especially with maintaining ministerial authority as its cornerstone, is principally conveyed through
the family motif so prevalent throughout his work. In several instances this image nearly operates as an artistic organizational
principle; sometimes it discloses facets of Edwards' thinking not
immediately evident at the expository level of a work. His reliance
on this motif, whether conscious or unconscious, represents a significant element in the tragedy of his career. Such traditional
images were still vital to him, still capable of conveying the emotional value they once held for early Puritans. To his parishioners,
however, these same images had become fossils of defunct verbal
conventions, mere words no longer vibrant with personal relevance. It is to Edwards' credit that at times he could breathe life
into this motif. Yet finally we are left with the impression that his
very language played a significant part in his defeat. For him the
family was nothing less than an archetypal image for the beautiful
order inherent in God's grand design. As the fundamental principle of all societies, it defined the relationship proper for all true
Christians among themselves as well as with regard to the role of
the minister as their spiritual father, and one of its basic features,
marriage, epitomized the bond between the regenerate soul and
Christ.

Edwards' fascination with the radiating circles of familial relations—family, church, town, nation, the collective self of history
and Christendom, the divine Self—is germane to his study of man's
inner being. Any sense of self-sufficiency or independence is reduced by this expanding context of identity. Curiously, however,
this radiation does not only dilate outward into the universe but
also opens inward upon the soul. Natural phenomena are real, in
one sense, but they are of value only as images or shadows of the
divine truth to be discerned within the self. Although nature reveals the divine Will, its disclosure actually becomes something of
a barrier between God and man, finally emphasizing the immense
distance between them. Man must apply his rational faculty to
penetrate nature's meaning—the law of reason and the law of na-

ture are identical—but reason, in its postlapsarian condition, is too feeble to give man much insight into God's design. Herein lies an explanation for the transformation of Edwards' youthful fascination with nature, for his movement away from the sort of empiricism one might expect from a student of Lockean thought. Though he never really lost his responsiveness to nature or abandoned certain lines of reasoning he learned from Locke, it cannot be safely argued that "Edwards was dramatically shifting the traditional emphasis: he was quoting Scripture to confirm the meaning of natural phenomena, not adducing natural images to confirm the meaning of Scripture."[5]

For Edwards nature's revelation of divine reality is less immediate, less vital, than the inner self's perception of it. He would have wholeheartedly agreed with Richard Henry Dana's resolution:

> "From nature up to nature's God," no more
> Grope out his way through parts, nor place before
> The Former the thing formed: Man yet shall learn
> The outward by the inward to discern,—
> The inward by the Spirit.[6]

For Edwards the two chief faculties of the self, understanding and the will, comprise the natural image of God and with special grace provide a direct communicative bond between the Deity and man. The theanthropic nature of Christ figured less prominently in Edwards' argument because he was interested less in the fact than in the actual experience of conversion. God's Spirit, dwelling within the saint's self, was what he sought to know. Consequently, he tended to internalize his images derived from nature in the sense that nature figures less in his writings as fact than as a source of types relating to the terrain of the heart. He had indeed realized the full implication of the thought he had expressed in his youthful notes on the mind when he had written, "*Within* and *Without*, are mere mental conceptions." Edwards' technique, as rudimentary as it is, adumbrates the portrait of the exterior world as a psychic

[5] Perry Miller makes this statement in *Images or Shadows of Divine Things*, p. 36. See also Conrad Cherry's reaction in *The Theology of Jonathan Edwards*, p. 46.
[6] *Poems and Prose Writings*, 1:386.

landscape or symbolic extension of the self in the writings of such American authors as Edgar Allen Poe, Nathaniel Hawthorne, and Herman Melville.

Edwards' stress on the immediate influence of special grace and the intuitive response of the heart closed the gap between God and man implied by nature. In focusing on the heart's intuition, he was careful not to deviate from the traditional Puritan view of the role of the understanding in the drama of conversion. His study of the conversion experience led him to conclude that the enlightenment of reason did not necessarily precede, in some demonstrable way, the turning of the heart as the traditional emphasis on a priori stages seemed to suggest. He was certain, however, that the illumination of this faculty always accompanied the indwelling of the Holy Spirit, that, strictly speaking, reason and the will never operated separately. What really mattered, what all Puritans had always agreed upon, was the turning of the heart. Thus, for Edwards, of the two ways of knowing, the one in accord with the Lockean notion of empiricism stressing sense perception receded in importance. He focused on the ability of the soul, independent of the sensorium, to detect intuitively the "inward sweetness" of grace. This was also how he interpreted the beatific vision, an experience in which saints received "an intuitive view of God": "This highest blessedness of the soul does not enter in at the door of the bodily senses; this would be to make the blessedness of the soul dependent on the body, or the happiness of man's superior part to be dependent on the inferior."[7]

It was in an effort to stimulate the intuitive perception of the hearts of his audience that Edwards conducted the rhetorical experiments we noted in some of his early writings. The use of paradoxically juxtaposed ascending and descending images in "The Excellency of Christ"; the lyrical passage depicting the eagle's flight at the end of "Jesus Christ Gloriously Exalted"; the incantatory, formulaic sentence patterns of *A Divine and Supernatural Light*; the distortion of the linear sequence of time in the "Personal Narrative"; the subtly interlocking strands of imagery in "The Future Punishment of the Wicked" and *Sinners in the Hands of an*

[7] *Works* (Dwight), 8:266, 264.

Angry God—such devices derived from Edwards' desire to communicate intuitively, at the level of felt experience. Thus, in spite of the rationality of his arguments, Edwards' style in these works does not reflect the neoclassical trend becoming more prominent during his time. The only instance of extensive punning in his work, for example, occurs at the conclusion of a sermon he delivered in 1740, entitled "Dishonesty." In his prefatory remarks to *Five Discourses*, there is in fact more than a hint of hostility to "such ornaments as politeness and modishness of style" and an "elegance of language" which were coming into vogue.[8] A respect for reason informed the neoclassical regard for style, and for Edwards reason was insufficient. It is appropriate, therefore, that stylistically he frequently frustrated the rational expectations of his audience. He believed it an error to think that "those preachers can't affect their hearers by enlightening their understandings, that don't do it by such a distinct, and learned handling of the doctrinal points of religion, as depends on human discipline, or the strength of natural reason." An appeal to the affections, to the intuitive perception of the heart, is just as important: "I think an exceeding affectionate way of preaching about the great things of religion, has in itself no tendency to beget false apprehensions of them; but on the contrary a much greater tendency to beget true apprehensions of them." What Edwards said of an affectionate method of delivery applies as well to the language of the sermon. Yet he never condoned slovenliness or lack of discipline. For him "method and order in [religious] discourses, for the help of the understanding and memory" are crucial.[9] Edwards' fondness for order always predominated in his own work. The important point to see, however, is his desire to achieve a balance between two extreme ways of preaching; method predominated in his own sermons, but it was a method which accommodated rhetorical experiments incorporating an appeal to the affections of his audience. He sought to arouse the whole man; through his rhetorical artistry he hoped to instruct the intellect and, as well, to move the will.

Edwards' penchant for the image of light is, as we have seen,

[8] Ibid., 5:349.
[9] The last three passages are from *Some Thoughts*, in Edwards, *The Great Awakening*, ed. C. C. Goen, p. 386.

likewise related to his regard for the intuitive perception of the heart. "Light is a strange work of God," he wrote in his notebook. "There [is] nothing in the whole external creation wherein appears a more admirable contrivance than this."[10] Light offered the best analogy or type he could find to convey what he meant by the intuition of the heart. His use of the image is not especially Newtonic; in fact, his references to the phenomenon of light must be judged superficial. In 1779 Ezra Stiles expressed the opinion in his diary that Edwards was a good scholar and a great metaphysician, "well skilled in the Logic of Ramus & Burgersdisius, & the philosophy of Wendeline, but not in Mathematics & the Ratiocinia of the Newtonian Philosophy."[11] However correct Stiles's observation may or may not be—it cannot be doubted that Edwards' reading of Newton made him particularly sensitive to certain lines of approach in argumentation and to certain images—Edwards' references to light clearly cannot be read as an indication of his modernity. Too frequently he was technically inaccurate when speaking of reflecting light, a primary example of which was a strange penchant to refer to the reflection of sunlight by the stars. Such passages, later emended by embarrassed editors who substituted the expression *luminary bodies* for the word *stars*, indicate Edwards' unconscious preference for an older cosmology than we find in Newton's work.[12] Aside from this curiosity, his use of the image actually shares a greater affinity with certain medieval traditions (by way of Saint John, Plotinus, and Saint Augustine) found in the works of, say, Robert Grosseteste, Roger Bacon, and Saint Bonaventure. In Grosseteste's *On Light and the Beginning of Forms*, for instance, God is presented as uncreated light from whence everything in creation derives in a sequence of diminishing illumination. When visible light reaches its maximum diffusion, it is reflected back to God (pure light). I am not suggesting by these remarks (the simplicity of which does injustice to Grosseteste's thesis) that Edwards was specifically indebted to medieval thinkers. Scripture alone, in such passages as 1 Tim. 6:16, could have encouraged his

[10] *The Philosophy of Jonathan Edwards*, p. 108.

[11] *Diary*, 2:337. See also Clarence H. Faust, "Jonathan Edwards as Scientist," *American Literature* 1 (January 1930): 393–404.

[12] See, for example, *Works* (Austin), 2:32, 95.

use of the image. I do mean that Edwards' fascination with the image, especially his use of it in the "Dissertation" in the ways we have observed, is more aligned with a tradition informed by medieval thinking than by Newton's empirical study. For Edwards the phenomenon of light has more to do with the spiritual than the physical realm: "this world is pleasant to us because the light is sweet, and the sensation is pleasant to the mind; how delightful a place then is heaven with its light, so much more fine, more harmonious, more bright."[13]

Light, for Edwards, not only symbolized the sense of the heart's intuition but also represented the radical order underlying everything, an order related to the beauty of God. In his notebooks he spoke of the traditional association of light and order, in one instance remarking through scriptural paraphrase that "when God began to make the world and put it into order and cause light to shine, it was a chaos, in a state of utter confusion, without form, and void, and darkness was upon the face thereof."[14] It is not surprising, then, that he described ministers, spiritual fathers maintaining family order, as luminaries. Ministers are "coworkers with Christ" and "the work of your minister is in some respects the same with the work of Christ," he explained in an ordination sermon delivered in 1749, entitled *Christ the Great Example of Gospel Ministers*. Edwards had in mind particularly the Christlike roles of priest and prophet. He was very cautious, to be sure, about the priestly office of the minister. Strictly speaking, "Ministers are not men's mediators," for Christ is the only true mediary who can intercede with God on man's behalf. Yet, "the work of ministers is in many respects like the work that Christ himself was appointed to, as the Saviour of men." The clergy do provide leadership in divine worship as well as administer the sacraments. In the sense that "ministers of the gospel, as Christ's servants and officers under him, are appointed to promote the designs of that great work of Christ, the work of salvation," they may be said to perform a priestly function.

Even more significant is the minister's role as prophet. In this capacity he is employed instrumentally by God to instruct men,

13 *Works* (Dwight), 8:534.
14 *Images or Shadows of Divine Things*, p. 70.

performing "the work which Christ does in his prophetical office; only with this difference, that ministers are to speak and act wholly under Christ, as taught of him, as holding forth his word, and by light and strength communicated from him."[15] The possession of this light signifies the alignment of the spiritual father with the Will of God. Such clergy are, as we noted earlier in *The True Excellency of a Minister of the Gospel*, "set by Christ to be lights or luminaries in the spiritual world"; "they are set to be that to men's souls, that the lights of heaven are to their bodies; and that they might be instruments and vehicles of God's greatest goodness, and the most precious fruits of his eternal love to them, and means of that life, and refreshment and joy, that are spiritual and eternal, and infinitely more precious than any benefit received by the benign beams of the sun in the firmament."

True ministers, in other words, are like the soul of the saint: when aligned with the divine Will they become, as it were, luminaries reflecting divine light back to God. Edwards' study of the drama of conversion led him to focus on the inner self as the best mirror of divine reality. Within the terrain of his sanctified heart, the saint intuitively perceives God's communicated light of grace. The mystical implications of this view are immediately apparent, but not in any simple sense. Edwards' mysticism is of the *catabatic* or reacting variety stressing communion or fellowship rather than union or oneness with God, the sanctification of the genuine self rather than the total loss of self.[16] Edwards staved off the conclusion that from this communion with God, from the bridging of the abyss between the saint and the Deity, arises a complete resolution of inward turmoil or an unwavering assurance of salvation. In contrast with the Quakers, who believed that the work of the Spirit within a convert can perfect him spiritually in this life, Edwards argues that while on earth the saint must undergo the progressive work of grace. This is why he warned in the sermon entitled "Great Care Necessary" that "those who entertain the opinion and

[15] The preceding quotations are from *Christ the Great Example of Gospel Ministers*, in *Works* (Austin), 8:375–395.

[16] My distinction is drawn from Adolf Deissmann, *Paul: A Study in Social and Religious History*, tr. William E. Wilson, pp. 147–157. The question of Edwards' mysticism, particularly as presented by Douglas Elwood, is discussed by Conrad Cherry in *The Theology of Jonathan Edwards*, pp. 87–88.

hope of themselves, that they are godly, should take great care to see that their foundation be right. Those that are in doubt should not give themselves rest till the matter is resolved."[17]

This comment pinpoints precisely the effect of the rhetorical techniques of the "Personal Narrative." Presumption is as dangerous as despair. God's ways with the soul are similar to His ways with history; divine meaning unfolds progressively. Thus the retrospective introspection of the saint is akin to the task of the historian, and just as the final stage of history "will be times of great peace and love," so too the soul will at last achieve an "inward quietness," something "of the tranquillity of heaven, the peace of the celestial paradise, that has the glory of God to lighten it."[18] The once paradisiacal terrain of the heart will eventually be fully restored through a regenerated childlike innocence, humility, and love. Until then, however, the saint must remain in time, in history, and struggle for peace within as well as without. As Edwards explained in a passage (noted earlier in our discussion) in which he typically internalizes nature, "The saints cannot always take comfort, and do not always taste the sweetness that there is in store for them, by reason of the darkness and clouds that sometimes interpose"; the intuitive inner glimpse they now and then "have of God in this world is like the twilight before sun-rising; it is not the direct light of the sun, but the light of the sun reflected, and it is comparatively a dim light." As they grow in gracious affections, such eclipses of the moonlike self diminish by degrees until "hereafter the saints shall enjoy the perfect day, they shall see God as we immediately behold the sun after it is risen above the horizon, and no cloud or vapour in the heavens to hinder its sight"; "how bright will their souls shine in the glorious image of God, made perfect in them . . . without anything to obscure the bright image."[19] As Edwards argued throughout "The Peace Which Christ Gives His True Followers," dated 1750, the brighter and more penetrating the reflected light of the self becomes, the greater and more secure is the saint's inward peace.

[17] *Works* (Austin), 8:69.

[18] *A History of the Work of Redemption*, in *Works* (Austin), 2:350; and "The Peace Which Christ Gives His True Followers," in ibid., 8:242.

[19] The preceding quotations are from an untitled sermon on Rom. 2:10, in *Works* (Dwight), 8:232, 266, 257.

By reasserting that uncertainty itself was a characteristic of the conversion process, Edwards solved the dilemma, expressed in his college diary, over his own spiritual experiences. Stages in the drama of conversion indeed occur, most evidently a posteriori rather than a priori ones, and spiritual unrest, in contrast to presumptuous complacency or desperate resignation, frequently may be interpreted as a sign of conversion. In a sense Edwards' entire career pivoted on this inner turmoil. His study of conversion became in effect spiritual autobiography. It furnished a way of defining his own experience, of determining whether he was saved. It is significant that the rigid, declarative voice declaiming the periodic sentences of *God Glorified* and *A Divine and Supernatural Light* gives way to a fluidity anticipated in "The Excellency of Christ" and the "Personal Narrative" and most effectively embodied in the cumulative sentences of the "Dissertation." Many of his earlier writings show Edwards' reluctance to identify too closely with his work; they reveal a distance protecting the author's self. The very apparent assertiveness, the very formality, of these works seems to disguise the young minister's inner wilderness of uncertainties. This separation is resolved in the later works, in which Edwards is more personally identifiable with the persona. Informing the style of the "Dissertation" is Edwards' somewhat mystical sense of the relation between the inner self and God. From the gentle, lucid, and enfolding prose of this work the reader receives a felt impression of what Edwards meant when he said that the saint's soul is "swallowed up" in God. Had he lived to rewrite *A History of the Work of Redemption* he would have produced the masterpiece he envisioned. More certain than ever before of a sense of identity between his inner self and the divine Self, Edwards would have even more perfectly realized his ministerial role as prophet.

In pursuing the question of his spiritual condition, Edwards had explored the inner self, discovering there reflections of the divine reality. The record of his successful quest for identity in Christ, the autobiography of his mind expressed in his writings, has rightly impressed many since his death. Not only his ideas but the artistic implications, however rudimentary, of his style and imagery equally deserve recognition as remarkable fruits harvested in the autumn of eighteenth-century New England Puritan culture.

Works Cited

Alexis, Gerhard T. "Jonathan Edwards and the Theocratic Ideal." *Church History* 35 (September 1966): 328–343.

Anderson, Wallace E. "Immaterialism in Jonathan Edwards' Early Philosophical Notes." *Journal of the History of Ideas* 25 (April 1964): 181–200.

Bercovitch, Sacvan. "Horologicals to Chronometricals: The Rhetoric of the Jeremiad." In *Literary Monographs, Volume Three*, pp. 1–124. Madison: University of Wisconsin Press, 1970.

Bostwick, David. *Self Disclaimed, and Christ Exalted*. London, 1759.

Bradstreet, Anne. *The Works of Anne Bradstreet*. Edited by Jeannine Hensley. Cambridge, Mass.: Harvard University Press, 1967.

Buckingham, Willis J. "Stylistic Artistry in the Sermons of Jonathan Edwards." *Papers in Language and Literature* 6 (Spring 1970): 136–151.

Bushman, Richard L. "Jonathan Edwards and Puritan Consciousness." *Journal for the Scientific Study of Religion* 5 (Fall 1966): 383–393.
———. "Jonathan Edwards as a Great Man: Identity, Conversion, and Leadership in the Great Awakening." *Soundings* 52 (Spring 1969): 15–46.

Cady, Edwin H. "The Artistry of Jonathan Edwards." *New England Quarterly* 22 (March 1949): 61–72.

Cherry, Conrad. *The Theology of Jonathan Edwards: A Reappraisal*. Garden City, N.Y.: Doubleday, 1966.

Cowan, James C. "Jonathan Edwards' Sermon Style: 'The Future Punishment of the Wicked Unavoidable and Intolerable.'" *South Central Bulletin* 29 (Winter 1969): 119–122.

Cremin, Lawrence A. *American Education: The Colonial Experience, 1607–1783*. New York: Harper & Row, 1970.

Crooker, Joseph H. "Jonathan Edwards: A Psychological Study." *New England Magazine* 2 (April 1890): 159–172.

Dana, Richard Henry. *Poems and Prose Writings.* 2 vols. New York: Baker & Scribner, 1850.

Davidson, Edward H. "From Locke to Edwards." *Journal of the History of Ideas* 24 (July 1963): 355–372.

———. *Jonathan Edwards: The Narrative of a Puritan Mind.* Cambridge, Mass.: Harvard University Press, 1968.

Deissmann, Adolf. *Paul: A Study in Social and Religious History.* Translated by William E. Wilson. New York: Harper, 1957.

Delattre, Roland André. *Beauty and Sensibility in the Thought of Jonathan Edwards.* New Haven: Yale University Press, 1968.

Dwight, Sereno E. *The Life of President Edwards.* Vol. 1. *The Works of President Edwards.* Edited by Sereno E. Dwight. 10 vols. New York: Carvill, 1830.

Edwards, Jonathan. "The Flying Spider—Observations by Jonathan Edwards When a Boy." Edited by Egbert C. Smyth. *Andover Review* 13 (January 1890): 5–13.

———. *Freedom of the Will.* Edited by Paul Ramsey. New Haven: Yale University Press, 1957.

———. *The Great Awakening.* Edited by C. C. Goen. New Haven: Yale University Press, 1972.

———. *Images or Shadows of Divine Things.* Edited by Perry Miller. New Haven: Yale University Press, 1948.

———. *Jonathan Edwards: Representative Selections.* Edited by Clarence H. Faust and Thomas H. Johnson. New York: Hill and Wang, 1962.

———. *Memoirs of the Rev. David Brainerd.* New Haven: Converse, 1822.

———. *"The Mind" of Jonathan Edwards: A Reconstructed Text.* Edited by Leon Howard. Berkeley: University of California Press, 1963.

———. *A Narrative and Defence of the Proceedings of the Ministers of Hampshire, Who Disapproved of Mr. Breck's Settlement at Springfield.* Boston, 1737.

———. *Original Sin.* Edited by Clyde A. Holbrook. New Haven: Yale University Press, 1970.

———. *The Philosophy of Jonathan Edwards.* Edited by Harvey G. Townsend. Eugene: University of Oregon Press, 1955.

———. *Religious Affections.* Edited by John E. Smith. New Haven: Yale University Press, 1959.

———. *An Unpublished Essay of Edwards on the Trinity.* Edited by G. P. Fisher. New York: Scribner's Sons, 1903.

———. "An Unpublished Letter by Jonathan Edwards." Edited by George Peirce Clark. *New England Quarterly* 29 (June 1956): 228–233.

———. *The Works of President Edwards.* Edited by Samuel Austin. 8 vols. Worcester, Mass., 1808–1809.

————. *The Works of President Edwards*. Edited by Sereno E. Dwight. 10 vols. New York: Carvill, 1830.

Faust, Clarence H. "Jonathan Edwards as Scientist." *American Literature* 1 (January 1930): 393–404.

Gaustad, Edwin Scott. *The Great Awakening in New England*. New York: Harper, 1957.

Gay, Peter. *A Loss of Mastery: Puritan Historians in Colonial America*. New York: Vintage, 1968.

Goen, C. C. "Jonathan Edwards: A New Departure in Eschatology." *Church History* 28 (March 1959): 25–40.

Grabo, Norman S. "Jonathan Edwards' *Personal Narrative*: Dynamic Stasis." *Literatur in Wissenschaft und Unterricht* 2 (1969): 141–148.

Heimert, Alan. *Religion and the American Mind: From the Great Awakening to the Revolution*. Cambridge, Mass.: Harvard University Press, 1966.

Holbrook, Clyde A. "Edwards and the Ethical Question." *Harvard Theological Review* 60 (April 1967): 163–175.

Holifield, E. Brooks. *The Covenant Sealed: The Development of Puritan Sacramental Theology in Old and New England, 1570–1720*. New Haven: Yale University Press, 1974.

Hooker, Thomas. *The Soules Implantation*. London, 1637.

————. *The Soules Vocation*. London, 1638.

Howard, Leon. "The Creative Imagination of a College Rebel: Jonathan Edwards' Undergraduate Writings." *Early American Literature* 5 (Winter 1971): 50–56.

Levin, David (ed.). *Jonathan Edwards: A Profile*. New York: Hill and Wang, 1969.

Lowance, Mason I., Jr. "Images or Shadows of Divine Things: The Typology of Jonathan Edwards." *Early American Literature* 5 (Spring 1970): 141–181.

Miller, Perry. *Errand into the Wilderness*. New York: Harper & Row, 1964.

————. *Jonathan Edwards*. New York: Sloane, 1949.

————. "Jonathan Edwards on the Sense of the Heart." *Harvard Theological Review* 41 (April 1948): 123–145.

————. " 'Preparation for Salvation' in Seventeenth-Century New England." *Journal of the History of Ideas* 4 (June 1943): 253–286.

————. "Solomon Stoddard, 1643–1729." *Harvard Theological Review* 34 (October 1941): 277–320.

———— and Thomas H. Johnson (eds.). *The Puritans: A Sourcebook of Their Writings*. 2 vols. New York: Harper & Row, 1963.

Morgan, Edmund S. *Visible Saints: The History of a Puritan Idea*. New York: New York University Press, 1963.

Morris, William S. "The Genius of Jonathan Edwards." *Reinterpretation in American Church History*. Edited by Jerold C. Brauer.

Chicago: University of Chicago Press, 1968.

Murdock, Kenneth B. *Literature and Theology in Colonial New England*. Cambridge, Mass.: Harvard University Press, 1949.

Pettit, Norman. *The Heart Prepared: Grace and Conversion in Puritan Spiritual Life*. New Haven: Yale University Press, 1966.

Piercy, Josephine K. *Studies in Literary Types in Seventeenth Century America (1607–1710)*. New Haven: Yale University Press, 1939.

Prince, Thomas (ed.). *Three Valuable Pieces*. Boston, 1747.

Schafer, Thomas. "Jonathan Edwards and Justification by Faith." *Church History* 20 (December 1951): 55–67.

———. "Solomon Stoddard and the Theology of the Revival." In *A Miscellany of American Christianity*, pp. 328–361. Durham, N.C.: Duke University Press, 1963.

Scheick, William J. "Anonymity and Art in *The Life and Death of That Reverend Man of God, Mr. Richard Mather*." *American Literature* 42 (January 1971): 457–467.

———. *The Will and the Word: The Poetry of Edward Taylor*. Athens: University of Georgia Press, 1974.

Shea, Daniel B., Jr. *Spiritual Autobiography in Early America*. Princeton: Princeton University Press, 1968.

Smith, Claude A. "Jonathan Edwards and 'The Way of Ideas.'" *Harvard Theological Review* 59 (April 1966): 153–174.

Stiles, Ezra. *The Literary Diary of Ezra Stiles*. Edited by Franklin Bowditch Dexter. 3 vols. New York: Scribner's Sons, 1901.

Stoddard, Solomon. *A Guide to Christ*. Boston, 1735.

———. *An Appeal to the Learned*. Boston, 1709.

———. *A Treatise Concerning Conversion*. Boston, 1719.

Tomas, Vincent. "The Modernity of Jonathan Edwards." *New England Quarterly* 25 (March 1952): 60–84.

Walsh, James P. "Solomon Stoddard's Open Communion: A Reexamination." *New England Quarterly* 43 (March 1970): 97–114.

Whittemore, Robert C. "Jonathan Edwards and the Theology of the Sixth Way." *Church History* 35 (March 1966): 60–75.

Winslow, Ola E. *Jonathan Edwards, 1703–1758: A Biography*. New York: Macmillan, 1940.

Index